A New Way of Eating...
A New Way of Living!

FIT FOR LIFE is a simple, natural diet embracing foods that work best together for optimal health. *A NEW WAY OF EATING FROM THE FIT FOR LIFE KITCHEN* will show you how to prepare, combine, and eat foods so that your body will deal with them quickly and effectively. More than just a health diet, this is a dietary adventure, featuring inventive, tempting, good-to-eat and good-for-you dishes, such as...

- POTATO LOVER'S SALAD. Trying to break the fried potato syndrome? Here's a winning combo of diced White Rose potatoes, steamed broccoli, and tangy garlic. Combined with Pea and Carrot Salad, it's a lightweight feast!

- TORTILLA BOOGIE. A mélange of asparagus, broccoli, yellow squash, cauliflower, Brussels sprouts, fresh mushrooms, and shredded greens, this corn tortilla is the ultimate in ~~...~~ eals.

- HONEY CORN ~~...~~ oney are the secret i ~~...~~ ome corn bread ever ~~...~~

Not to mention fr ~~...~~ ng soups and sandwiches, meals for weekend and holiday feasts, perfect breads and grains, easy vegetable pies and pastries, great chow mein, egg rolls, and tempting tempura, too!

Books by
Marilyn and Harvey Diamond

FIT FOR LIFE
FIT FOR LIFE II: LIVING HEALTH
THE AMERICAN VEGETARIAN COOKBOOK
FROM THE FIT FOR LIFE KITCHEN

Published by
WARNER BOOKS

A NEW WAY OF EATING

FROM THE FIT FOR LIFE *KITCHEN*

MARILYN DIAMOND

WARNER BOOKS

A Time Warner Company

WARNER BOOKS EDITION

Cover photograph by Pat York

Illustrations by Marilyn Diamond

Warner Books, Inc.
1271 Avenue of the Americas
New York, NY 10020

Ⓦ A Time Warner Inc. Company

Printed in the United States of America

Originally published in trade paperback by Warner Books.

First Mass Market Printing: September, 1993

10 9 8 7 6 5 4 3

CONTENTS

CONTENTS

WHAT IS HEALTH

HEALTH is a synergistic or cooperative process whereby all human experience, that of the body, the mind, and the spirit, is enhanced. Every way that you meet your environment, all your physical, intellectual, and psychological actions, interactions, and reactions, is increasingly positive. HEALTH is not static. It is an ongoing condition of constant improvement. Through proper nourishment of your physical body and sufficient exercise—which the body naturally craves if it is nourished properly—excess weight ceases to be a problem, and the emotional, intellectual, and spiritual blockages that frequently accompany it no longer exist. HEALTH is your birthright. It is the normal state of being, not the exception. This book has been written to show you how it is possible for you personally to attain HEALTH and to depend on the "inner physician" deep inside all of us. HEALTH means self-sufficiency, self-knowledge, and the ability to adjust one's individual circumstances in order to experience life at the highest possible level.

WHAT IS HEALTH

INTRODUCTION

I used to think that the only way I could have a "fancy gourmet" meal was if I couldn't pronounce the chef's name. As far as getting a *healthy* gourmet meal, well, that I never even thought possible. Marilyn proved me wrong on both counts.

When I first met Marilyn she had already had an extensive background in gourmet cookery, having traveled a good part of the world and studied with various teachers. *I* had an extensive background in eating. With the knowledge that food played an extremely important role in our health we very much wanted to be able to eat exciting, delicious food that was relatively simple to prepare but a gustatory delight. *Plus*, it had to meet the needs of the body and support health.

Marilyn, being a genius in the kitchen, went right to work perfecting some phenomenally great tasting food which she tested on *me*. The only person who possibly could have been in a higher state of bliss would have been a kid turned loose in a toy store able to have *anything* he or she wanted.

I could hardly believe some of the spectacular meals I was eating that actually helped me *maintain* the health and weight loss I had achieved. I've eaten every recipe in this book, and after you have done the same you will see why I am so enthusiastic and excited about it. We are both extremely pleased that these recipes are being made available to everyone.

This is fabulous food. It looks good, it smells good, it tastes good, and it is good for you. You just can't beat that kind of combination. Enjoy!

Harvey Diamond

PREFACE

We hear more and more these days about the dangers of certain foods and the importance of correct eating habits to prevent disease and maintain optimum health. People are becoming increasingly aware of the need to make changes in their diets, but what changes and how to affect them are questions frequently asked—particularly in light of so much contradictory nutritional information. I wrote this book in 1980 as a practical companion to *The Totally Healthy Person: A Case For Health*, written by my husband, Harvey. His book attempted to resolve contradictions about diet and its effect on health. My book was intended to offer answers to the questions people were asking about *how* to change their diets. Six years later, the simple principles illustrated in this work have been formally structured into the program we call *Fit For Life*. Many of you, having read *Fit For Life*, may already be aware of these basic principles, but since we find that with new information, "repetition is the mother of perfection," a brief review will perhaps help to make this little book more useful to you.

There are several dietary principles to keep in mind as you go through this book. The first principle stresses the introduction of a sufficient quantity of *water-content food* into your diet. The only foods that contain this vital water are fruits and vegetables in their natural state. One of my goals in writing this book was to help people make the transition to live, water-content food. You can appreciate the importance of making this transition when you consider that this planet and our bodies are predominantly water and in order to maintain health and harmony, our diets must consist of foods that are also predominantly water in their composition.

The second principle upon which this book is based is that of *proper food combining*. I have designed the recipes in this book to show you how to prepare and eat foods in such a way that they will not hinder one another's passage through the digestive tract. You will find many examples of how to prepare and combine foods correctly so that your body will be able to deal with them quickly and effectively, and so that you will not experience a heavy feeling after eating. Your body will also be receiving the optimum nutrition from what you are eating, since food will not be spoiling in your digestive tract before nutrients can be absorbed. Proper food combining is crucial to good health. Once you have learned how to properly combine what you eat, you will be amazed at how much lighter and better you feel. (Turn to the back of this book to find out how you can obtain a Fit For Life Proper Food Combining Chart.)

The third important principle I emphasize in this book is the correct consumption of fruit. Fruit, if eaten properly, is the most cleansing food you can eat. It helps to wash away the obstructions and blockages in your body that have built up over the years because of the insufficient consumption of water-content food, improper food combining, and the lack of adequate exercise.

If HEALTH, including proper body weight, is now your goal, this book will help you to make the changes in diet necessary to realize that goal. For some the transition may take only a short time. For others, it may be a more long-range aim. It is not the speed but the direction that is important.

In all the recipes you will find in the following pages, only the finest quality, purest ingredients are recommended. If you are serious about improving your health and losing excess weight, you will want to avoid processed foods containing chemical preservatives and additives. In order to receive the highest quality nourishment from fresh, wholesome meals, you must use the best, freshest, least refined ingredients available.

When you think of a balanced diet from now on, think of balancing the amount of live, water-content food you eat with the cooked food that you eat. The quantity of water-content food, *uncooked*, (fresh juices, fruit, and salads), should predominate. That is what *we* mean by a balanced diet. We reject the "four food groups" approach, finding it to be an antiquated and physiologically unsound hypothesis presented to the public more out of a concern to satisfy commercial interests than for its effectiveness in terms of our health. The "four food lobbies" would be a more correct label. That for decades we have followed the advice to eat *at every meal* meat, dairy, grain, and fruits or vegetables in the name of "balancing" our diets has resulted in 90 percent of the population being overweight and in annual expenditures of billions of dollars in stomach medications and digestive aids. The overemphasis on animal protein, in particular, has resulted in widespread protein poisoning. Overweight, cellulite, irritability, depression, and skin problems are its most obvious manifestations. Clearly, it is time to balance our diets in a new way!

Thus you will find the emphasis in this book to be on menus that help you cut down on protein and dairy, lowering your consumption of animal fat and increasing your consumption of fruits and vegetables, all right in line with current dietary guidelines.

I designed this book to take you on a dietary adventure ranging from light, cleansing fruit and vegetable juices to feasts of vegetable turnovers, pies, or crescents. There is something for everybody here. I thought often during my writing of the many people who asked, "How do I live on a predominantly fruit and vegetable diet and not become bored?" and I took great care not to disappoint them. For those who are already familiar with *Fit For Life*, you will notice some recipes here that are similar, though frequently simpler than those in *Fit For Life*. Most of the recipes in this book are the original, less involved versions, created eight to ten years ago, when I was first developing a high-water-content, properly combined cuisine. As I go through this book now to update it for publication in 1987, I have chosen to leave it in its present form so that it can be used as it was originally intended, as a simple, handy manual to guide you in your use of the principles. Thus, it is actually *more* than a cookbook, and the recipes are easy illustrations of the principles, which you can tailor to your personal tastes and life-style. The feedback we have received from the thousands of people who already have this book is that it is a very useful support to the *Fit For Life* program, which convinces us that even though it was written eight years in advance of *Fit For Life*, it is still totally relevant. This book holds great memories of the early years, when Harvey and I were working together on this program and so much of what I prepared at mealtime was conceptually new. I remember vividly Harvey's great enthusiasm and excitement over all these different, predominantly vegetable dishes! It was so gratifying and inspiring! What you will find in this book is my kitchen diary from the years when I was developing a new way of eating on our journey to HEALTH. Now it becomes *your* journey. You can take as long as you desire, knowing you are on the right road, and by all means *have a great time*. We certainly did! And we continue to do so, since the road to health is a journey that never ends.

Marilyn Diamond

BEWARE OF ACID-FORMING FOODS

Many of the foods eaten on a routine basis have the deleterious effect of acidifying the system. An acid system is an unhealthy system. The delicate inner linings of the digestive tract are under constant caustic assault. The body, always endeavoring to maintain its integrity, stores great quantities of water to dilute these acids so that the vital organs will not be harmed. Thus the first visible effect of an acid system is water retention, bloat, and distended upper arms and thighs, or what is commonly called cellulite. Other results of acid in the system are hair loss, graying hair, and dark bags under the eyes. Poor eyesight and hearing, loss of calcium from the teeth and bones, extreme tension or nervousness—all are manifestations of excess acidity.

The following are flagrant causes of acid in your body: meat, coffee, alcohol, dairy products, cooked nuts, cooked fruit, and chemically processed foods, such as white sugar, white flour, and all foods treated with chemical preservatives. In addition, smoking causes great quantities of acid in the system. It is no accident that we do not emphasize any of these substances in the diet for HEALTH. We offer delicious alternatives that you can substitute for them. We suggest ways to avoid the premature aging that is the result of an acid condition. Fresh fruit and vegetable juices neutralize acid, since their effects are alkaline in your system. Although many fruits are acid by classification, all fruits are alkaline in the body and only become acid if they are cooked or are eaten with or *on top of* other food. Following the recommendations in this book, you will be able to avoid acidifying your body and you will learn to neutralize acidity when it does occur. When you do include acid-forming foods, such as meat and dairy, in your diet, you will know how to properly combine them to minimize their harmful effects.

1
FRESH JUICES

Nature's Power Foods

Fresh fruit and vegetable juices are the crucial ingredients of an elimination diet. They work together for your well-being. Fruit juices are a concentrated energy food. Their natural sugars stir up and flush out accumulated waste and toxic material. Vegetable juices expedite the eliminative process and provide the necessary elements for rebuilding healthy blood, bones, and tissue. From fresh juices you receive the most benefit with the least expenditure of body energy.

Fresh fruit and vegetable juices are useful tools in the quest for HEALTH. If it is at all possible, acquire one of the many fruit and vegetable juicers on the market. Considering the health benefits you will receive from the juices they provide, these wonderful machines are comparatively inexpensive. Sturdy and adequate models retail for around $125.00. Simple electric citrus juicers cost much less (from $15 to $30) and are also extremely important.

You cannot compare any of the bottled varieties to fresh-squeezed juice. The shelf life for juice is limited. The longer it stands, the more it loses its vital elements. For maximum benefits, you should consume your juice immediately after preparing it. Avoid the consumption of pasteurized juices, which are denatured through heating and are *acid-forming* as a result.

Fruit and vegetable juices work together for your well-being. Fruit juices stir up and flush out accumulated toxins. Their concentrated natural sugars bring you vital energy and speed up the eliminative process. Vegetable juices provide the important elements for rebuilding healthy blood, bones, and tissue.

Whenever possible, consume nothing but fruit juice or fresh fruit in the morning. Although you have been led to believe that a large breakfast is necessary for energy in the morning, common sense must tell you that the energy to *digest* that large breakfast has to come from somewhere. It comes from the not unlimited supply of vital energy that you have at your disposal. That is why two hours after people consume breakfast, they are "dying" for a cup of coffee to keep them going. They have dissipated all their energy in digestion. Fruit juice and fruit, on the other hand, supply your body with *real* energy. During digestion, everything eaten must be transformed into glucose. Fruit juice is fructose, and the transformation process from fructose to glucose requires very little energy from your body. That is why we say that fruit juice supplies you with real energy—instant natural sugar that your body can put to immediate use.

If you drink nothing but fruit juice in the morning, you relieve your body of the work required to digest a heavier breakfast. This frees up vital energy for other important activities. (Even a so-called "light" breakfast of only toast and coffee saps much of your body energy for digestion. Coffee is extremely heavy, and only one cup takes twenty-four hours to pass through the kidneys.) If you wish to eat something heavier than juice in the morning, let it be only fruit. Once you have made the transition from your usual breakfast to a juice or fruit breakfast, you will be amazed at how much more energy you will have at your disposal in the morning. You will also find that you will begin to lose the excess weight you have been wrestling with for so long. During the mornings when you consume only juice or fruit, your body can expend energy on eliminating excess weight, since it does not have to work on digestion.

Any of the following fruits make cleansing and energizing juices:

Apple—It is not necessary to peel the apples, but it is important to core them.

Orange—You can peel the oranges and put them through a vegetable juicer, which results in a thick, frothy juice. Or you can cut the oranges in half and juice them on a citrus juicer.

Grapefruit—Prepare the same way as orange juice.

Pineapple—Cut the skin from the pineapple and put large chunks through a juicer. You do not have to remove the core.

Grape—Put any type of grape through the juicer. The seeds will be collected with the pulp. Grape juice is particularly concentrated, so you may want to use half grape and half apple.

Watermelon—Remove the rind and put chunks of watermelon through a juicer. This is an extremely cleansing and refreshing juice.

Cantaloupe—Remove the rind and the seeds and put chunks of cantaloupe through a juicer.

Honeydew—Prepare the same way as cantaloupe juice. There are many possible fruit juice combinations:

Apple-grape
Orange-grapefruit
Pineapple-orange
Watermelon-cantaloupe-honeydew

If ever you crave a heavier juice, try apple-banana or pineapple-banana. Put a banana through a juicer and then put the juicier fruit through to wash out the thick banana juice. This is an extremely satisfying drink in the morning.

There is one rule that is important to remember regarding juices: *Always consume fruit juices ON AN EMPTY STOMACH.* They serve to wash or cleanse the system, in addition to supplying immediate vital energy. If they are poured into a stomach full of food, they cannot pass through and they ferment. In addition, the digestive process is immediately aborted as the digestive enzymes are diluted. This rule applies to both fruit and vegetable juices. You must allow at least two hours after a meal before drinking juice.

If you have been accustomed to drinking alcoholic beverages before meals, substitute a glass of fresh fruit or fresh vegetable juice. This opens up the digestive passages and aids in the digestion of the meal. Alcohol has an aging effect because of the acid and fermentation it causes in the system. In that they are cleansing and the suppliers of the important elements for rebuilding body tissue, fresh fruit and vegetable juices are rejuvenating.

The following are examples of some excellent vegetable juices:

Carrot—This is perhaps the most important of all the vegetable juices. It is the basis for all other vegetable juices that I recommend. You do not need to scrape the carrots. Simply wash them well and remove the stems. Do not heed the misinformed who tell you that carrot juice will turn you orange. If there is a slight yellowing of the palms when you start to drink large quantities of carrot juice, it is due to the cleansing of the excess bile from your liver. The bile causes the temporary discoloration until it is washed away by the bloodstream. The slight discoloration has nothing to do with the carotene in the carrots and is actually a sign of returning or increasing health.

Carrot-celery—If you are preparing 12 ounces of juice, 3 ounces should be celery and the remaining 9 ounces should be carrot. This is an extremely important juice for your transition diet. The high alkalinity of the celery neutralizes the acid build-up in your body from smog, smoking, alcohol, meat, coffee, sugar, and all processed foods. If you are trying to give up meat or coffee and you do have a meal that includes these, *be sure* to have a large carrot-celery juice *on an empty stomach* the next day to help neutralize the acidity. This juice is also helpful in neutralizing the acids resulting from dairy product consumption. If you are trying to give up smoking, a habit that makes your body chemistry *extremely* acid, drink carrot-celery juice, which will neutralize the acid condition. The less acid you are, the fewer cigarettes you will crave. If you are making the transition from a meat-eating diet to a vegetarian diet, it is recommended that you drink at least one large glass of carrot-celery juice every day.

Carrot-celery-spinach-lettuce—Three to 4 ounces of the green juice, 8 to 9 ounces of the carrot juice. This juice has strong laxative (cleansing) effects. The organic oxalic acid in the spinach facilitates the peristaltic action in the intestines. If you suffer from constipation, this juice will help you enormously. Celery is a source of natural sodium chloride and will help you to cut down on your salt intake, and if you have the occasion to spend time in an exceedingly hot climate, celery juice can help you to withstand the heat.

Carrot-cucumber-beet—Three ounces of cucumber (peeled), 1 of beet, and 8 ounces of carrot is a good blend.

Combination vegetable juice—Combine in whatever amounts are most tasteful to you any of the following vegetables: carrot, celery, tomato, spinach, parsley, green or red pepper, lettuce, cucumber, or beets.

No matter what diet you are following, fresh fruit and vegetable juices can become an important part of it. Be sure to consume these juices properly: *on an empty stomach,* not with or immediately after meals. Fruit juices are the cleansers of the human system. Vegetable juices are the builders and regenerators of the body. When you add them to your diet, you will immediately begin to feel their positive effects.

SMOOTHIES—FOR FUN

Smoothies are combination fruit drinks that are made in a blender. Since they include the pulp, they are thicker than regular fruit juices and are therefore more filling. Children of all ages love smoothies. Substitute them for dairy drinks such as milkshakes, which are highly mucus-forming.

Because they are made exclusively of fruit, they are cleansing and energizing.

Any of a number of fruits can be combined in a smoothie. Usually one or two bananas are used to lend a thick consistency. The banana can be fresh or frozen. If you are planning on using frozen bananas for smoothies, simply peel them, place them in a plastic bag, and leave them for several hours in the freezer. The recipes below are examples of some popular smoothies, but they are certainly not the only possibilities. Use your favorite fruits and experiment.

APPLE-DATE SMOOTHIE

```
        2  bananas, fresh or frozen
        2  apples, peeled and cored
2 to 4  large dates, seeds removed
        1  cup fresh apple juice
```

Whirl all the ingredients in a blender until smooth.

STRAWBERRY-PAPAYA SMOOTHIE

```
6 to 7  strawberries, fresh or frozen
     1  papaya, scooped out of the skin
     1  frozen banana
     1  cup fresh orange juice
```

Whirl all the ingredients in a blender until smooth.

APRICOT-PEACH SMOOTHIE

2 peaches, seeds removed, peeled if desired
4 apricots, seeds removed
2 bananas, fresh or frozen
½ cup fresh orange juice or apple juice

Whirl all the ingredients in a blender until smooth.

BLUEBERRY SMOOTHIE

1 cup blueberries
2 peaches, seeds removed, peeled if desired
1 frozen banana
1 cup orange juice or apple juice

Whirl all the ingredients in a blender until smooth.

MELON SMOOTHIE

1 cup watermelon
1 cup honeydew
1 cup cantaloupe

Whirl all the ingredients in a blender until smooth. Some or all of the melon can be frozen, if desired, for a colder, thicker drink.

2

FRUIT AND FRUIT SALADS

The Body's Cleansing Agents

*"A day without fruit is a day without sunshine,"
but fruit must never be combined with other
foods. Eaten alone, on an empty stomach, it
can proceed directly to the intestines, where it
is digested. If fruit is eaten in this way, it is the
least fattening, most cleansing food on this
planet. Fruit has the highest water content of
any food, and its natural sugars act as a
detergent, washing away stored excesses and
waste matter that are clogging the system.*

FRUIT AND FRUIT SALADS

Fruit *as a rule* must be eaten by itself. It carries with it its own digestive enzymes and digests in the intestines, passing quickly through the stomach. With the exception of bananas, avocados, and dried fruits, all fruits want to go directly to the intestines. If they are eaten in combination with other foods, their speedy digestion is impeded and they ferment in the stomach, where they do not belong, causing bloat and acid indigestion.

The reason that most people have the sad misconception that fruit is fattening is that they do not eat it at the proper time. And they usually combine it with other foods. Fruit, when eaten alone *on an empty stomach,* is the least fattening, most cleansing food available on this planet. Its all-important water content is the highest of any food. Its natural sugars act as a detergent in the system, washing away stored excesses and waste matter. When you are cleansing your system, using fruit as the cleansing agent, do not make the mistake of cluttering yourself up first with a quantity of other foods before you eat the fruit. When you are empty (as in the mornings) and ready to eat, reach for fruit (or fruit juice) *before anything else* so that it can go through first and wash your system.

The great variety of fruits available makes the preparation of fruit salads an experience that can always have an element of surprise. Whenever it is possible, seek out organically grown fruit that has not been sprayed with pesticides. Although organic fruit is not always uniform and perfect to the eye, it more often than not has a better flavor and consistency than the mass-produced variety.

Some of the fruits I list below may not be available in your region. Make use of whatever is available to you *in season,* for whatever is in season at the time will be freshest. For example, most apples that are available in the spring have been stored since the fall. A fruit salad can be delicious with only three or four different fruits in it.

Be careful that you do not combine fruit salads with any other food. Make them large enough so that they will be satisfying as an entire meal. Eat a large fruit salad for breakfast, and you will be amazed at how much *real* energy you feel. It cannot be compared to the buzz you receive from coffee in the morning, which is an unnatural stimulation and costly to the body. The rush you feel when you consume a cup of coffee is in actuality the result of your body speeding itself up to rid itself of a substance it recognizes as harmful.

A large fruit salad makes a perfect lunch or evening meal in the warm summer months. If, on occasion, you wish to have your fruit salad as part of a meal, combining it, for example, with hot bran muffins, be sure that you eat the fruit salad *first, before* the bran muffins. *Never under any circumstances eat fruit or fruit salad directly after a meal!* You will deprive yourself of its cleansing benefits, and unless your system is totally insensitized after years of abuse, you will probably experience discomfort and indigestion as the fruit ferments in your stomach.

SPRING-SUMMER FRUIT SALADS

Apricots	Figs	Peaches
Bananas	Grapes	Pineapples
Blackberries	Honeydew	Plums
Blueberries	Kiwi fruit	Prunes
Cantaloupe	Mangoes	Raspberries
Cherries	Nectarines	Strawberries
Crenshaw	Papayas	Watermelon

Combine any of the above fruits. Although in proper food combining, melons are eaten alone and not in combination with any other fruit, when you are first beginning to change your diet, you may wish to add melon to your fruit salads. As your taste buds become more sensitive, you will probably begin to enjoy melons most when you eat them by themselves.

Certain summer fruits make excellent sauces for fruit salads. To make the sauces, you puree the fruits in a blender and then pour them over the fruit salad. The following make excellent sauces:

Banana-peach	Peach-apricot
Mango	Strawberry-banana
Mango-papaya	Strawberry-papaya
Papaya-fig	

You can experiment with other possible fruit salad sauces. Fresh orange juice also makes a good sauce.

FALL-WINTER FRUIT SALADS

Apples	Grapefruit	Pears
Bananas	Grapes	Persimmons
Dates	Indian red peaches	Raisins
Dried figs	Kiwi fruit	Tangelos
Dried prunes	Oranges	Tangerines
Figs	Papayas	

Raisins are an important addition to fall-winter fruit salads. They supply concentrated fruit sugar, which is a little harder to come by in the winter than in the summer.

Pears in the blender make an excellent sauce for winter fruit salads, or you can combine pears, bananas, and raisins in the blender. One of the most elegant sauces can be made from persimmons. When they are ripe, they have the natural consistency of a sauce and need only be peeled and mixed in with the salad.

Use dried fruits sparingly. They are extremely concentrated, and people have a tendency to overeat on them. It is usually advisable to soak dried fruit for a short time to restore some of the moisture before eating it. If you are going to add dried fruit to your fruit salads, chop it.

The possibilities in preparing fruit salads are endless. Below are a few samples of some extremely successful combinations.

TROPICAL FRUIT SALAD

1 large navel orange
1 large ripe mango (or 2 or 3 small ones)
1 papaya
1 pint fresh strawberries
1 apple (for crispness)
2 bananas
1 cup fresh pineapple chunks
2 Tbs. freshly grated coconut

Peel the orange and slice it across the sections into wheels. Peel the mango and cut the fruit off the seed. Cut the papaya in half, remove the seeds, and peel it. Cut the fruit into chunks. Slice the strawberries. Peel, core, and dice the apple. Add peeled, sliced bananas and pineapple chunks. Mix all the fruit well in a large bowl. Top with grated coconut. This fruit salad conjures up warm breezes and palm trees no matter where you are.

Remember to eat it on an empty stomach! If these tropical fruits are hard to find in your area, there may be a specialty shop that sells them. The cost will be well worth the pleasure of eating it and the benefits you will receive from it. Serves 2 for a weekend brunch or lunch or a summer evening meal.

KIWI FRUIT SALAD

2 to 4 kiwi fruit, depending on the size
   1 large bosc pear
  ½ pint fresh strawberries
   1 large navel orange
   1 cup red emperor grapes, halved, with the seeds removed
   1 papaya
   1 large banana
   2 Tbs. freshly grated coconut

Peel the kiwi fruit and cut them into rounds. Peel and core the pear and dice it. Slice the strawberries. Peel the orange and slice it across the sections into wheels. Add the grapes. Cut the papaya in half, remove the seeds, peel it, and slice it. Add the peeled, sliced banana. Mix all the fruit well in a large bowl. Top with grated coconut. This is enough for breakfast or lunch for 1 to 2 people.

WINTER FRUIT SALAD

  2 bananas
  2 crisp apples
  1 large pear
  2 tangerines
  1 large navel orange
  1 large persimmon, ripe to the soft stage
  ½ cup raisins, soaked for ½ hour in warm water

Peel and slice the bananas. Peel, core, and cube the apples. Peel and core the pear and slice it. Add the tangerines, peeled and sectioned. Peel the orange and slice it across the sections into wheels. Add the persimmon. If it is ripe enough, it should form a thick sauce. Add the raisins. Mix all the fruit well in a large bowl. Serves 2.

A WORD ABOUT COOKED FRUIT

As you go through the recipes in this book, you are going to notice an absence of any recipes calling for cooked fruit. "Well, what is wrong with cooked fruit?" you ask. Everything! In its natural state, fruit is without doubt the most cleansing, life-supporting food you can consume. But when it is organically altered by heat, its benefits are lost and instead of having a beneficial effect it has a highly acid effect on your system. Acid degenerates whatever it comes into contact with, and the acid in your body resulting from improper dietary habits does a great deal of damage to your sensitive inner organs. It is unlikely that you would deliberately pour acid on your skin. It is important that you do not cause acid to come into contact with the delicate linings of your inner tissues as well.

A common error made is that of referring to fruits as acidic because they are classified as acid fruits. *All* fruit is alkaline in the body and works to neutralize the acids in your system resulting from wrong eating habits. Fruit only becomes acid if cooked before eaten. In that case, instead of aiding in rebalancing your inner chemistry, it only serves to aggravate the problem. So by all means, eat fruit in abundance, but *leave cooked fruit alone*.

A WORD ABOUT NUTS

Nuts are an extremely concentrated food, and they require a fairly clear digestive tract for the body to obtain the most benefit from them. So many people overeat on nuts that we do not recommend that they be incorporated into most transition diets. If you cannot limit your nut intake to a small handful a day, then it is best to leave them alone. Eating too many results in an overworked system, and then few of their nutritional benefits can be reaped.

It is imperative when eating nuts to eat only raw ones. Cooked nuts have been organically altered and are therefore extremely acid-forming. Raw almonds are the most nutritious. Next in order of their value are pecans, pine nuts, black walnuts, butternuts, beechnuts, English walnuts, and filberts. Peanuts are to be avoided. They are not nuts at all but legumes, which are particularly destructive to the human system when dried, because of their extreme acid action and low water content.

If you are going to eat nuts, there are two recommended ways to do so. You can have them as a light lunch or snack with cucumber or celery, or you can make them into nut milks by liquefying them in a blender using 1 part nuts to 4 parts water. The recipe for nut and seed milks is included in *Fit For Life*.

3

VEGETABLE SALADS

The Building Blocks
for Regeneration

"A salad a day keeps the doctor away," and
allowing yourself to become "addicted" to
salad is one of the best steps you can take on
your new diet. With the exception of juicy
fruit, there is no other food that contains the
necessary water content for optimum body
functioning and weight control.

THE BASIC EVERYDAY SALAD

The amounts indicated below will make a large salad for 2 or 3 people.

- 1 head lettuce—iceberg or head, romaine, Boston or butter, red leaf, salad bowl, Bibb, or some of each
- 1 bunch spinach (optional)
- 2 to 3 ripe tomatoes, or 1 pint cherry tomatoes
- 1 cucumber
- 2 to 3 cups sprouts—alfalfa, red clover, mung bean, lentil, sunflower, etc.

Wash and drain the lettuce and the spinach. Chop or break the lettuce into bite-sized pieces in a large wooden salad bowl. Finely chop the spinach and add it to the lettuce. (The spinach is more efficiently digested if it is chopped.) Cut the tomatoes into bite-sized chunks, peel and slice the cucumber, and add these to the greens. Unless you are using the European or hothouse variety, you should always peel cucumbers because they are waxed. Add the sprouts.

Fresh sprouts are the most important ingredient in your salad. On page 69 of *Survival into the 21st Century,* Viktoras Kulvinskas explains, "The chemical changes which occur in the sprouting seed activate a powerful enzyme factory which is never surpassed at any later stage of growth. This rich enzyme concentration induces a heightened enzyme activity in your metabolism leading to regeneration of the bloodstream and digestive processes."

If you wish to have the freshest sprouts possible, you can grow your own at home. This is a simple four-day process, accomplished in a large sprouting jar with a wire-mesh lid, which can be purchased at your local natural foods store. Alfalfa, mung bean, or lentil are among the easiest to grow, and seeds for these are usually available where you purchase the sprouter, along with easy-to-follow directions.

Your new diet should include a basic salad at least once a day. The basic salad combines well with proteins (meat, poultry, fish, eggs, cheese, nuts, or seeds) and with carbohydrates (bread, grains, and potatoes). It is the perfect accompaniment to plain or fancy vegetable dishes. It also combines well with many of the heavier salad recipes that appear later on in this section.

The importance of eating a salad each day cannot be overemphasized. With the exception of juicy fruit, no other part of your diet will contain the necessary water-content food required for optimum body functioning and weight control. Remember that you are mostly water and that you are working toward a diet that is predominantly water-content food.

You can vary your daily basic salad by adding desired amounts of any of the following *raw* vegetables:

Asparagus tips	Jerusalem artichokes
Beets	Mushrooms
Broccoli	Peas
Cabbage	Radishes (These are irritating
Carrots	to the digestive system
Cauliflower	and therefore should be
Celery	eaten with discretion.)
Corn	Zucchini

These raw vegetables can be thinly sliced, finely grated, or put through a food processor. They add substance and variety to your basic salad and help to make it a satisfying meal.

THE BASIC SALAD DRESSING

2 to 3 Tbs. fresh-squeezed lemon juice
⅓ to ½ cup unrefined oil (olive, safflower, sesame, sunflower, or avocado)

Whenever you are using oil, use the unrefined, cold-pressed variety, for it is the most easily digested. Hydrogenated oils cannot be assimilated by the body and cause blockages in the system.

Whip the oil and lemon together for a creamy dressing.

If desired, the following seasonings can be added to the Basic Salad Dressing:

¼ to ½ tsp. sea salt—Beware of the amount of salt you eat. Its deleterious effects will slow down your progress toward HEALTH. If you find that you are craving salt, one way that you can lessen the craving is to cut down on your starch intake. Too much salt in the diet causes a water-logged condition. If you are going to use a small amount of salt, be sure that it is natural sea salt, rather than chemically processed "iodized" salt. Sea salt can be found in all natural foods stores and most supermarkets.

¼ to ½ tsp. seasoned salt—Spike is one of the best seasoned salts I have ever used and can be found in most supermarkets and natural foods stores. There are many seasoned salts on the market. Make sure that the one you buy is totally free of chemical additives.

1 tsp. to 1 Tbs. tamari—A concentrated soy sauce that is quite salty and should be used sparingly.

1 clove garlic—Although to most people garlic tastes delicious, there are several reasons you should not use it all the time. First, it is irritating to the sensitive lining of the digestive tract. Second, it has the effect of overstimulating the taste buds, causing you to crave heavier and heavier foods. (Onions, scallions, shallots, and leeks have the same effect.) If you wish to use garlic in your salad, one way to do so is to rub your wooden salad bowl with it before adding the greens.

¼ to 1 tsp. herbs—These can be fresh or dried. Oregano, basil, thyme, tarragon, parsley, and bouquet garni, which is a blend of several herbs, are some of the nice ones. Do not overuse herbs to the point where they camouflage natural flavors of other foods. You do not need much to enjoy their flavors, especially if you rub them between your fingers as you add them to your salad. This crushing helps to release the flavors.

1 to 2 Tbs. mayonnaise—If you wish to include mayonnaise in your dressing for its creamy effect, be sure that you are using a mayonnaise that does not contain sugar. Most commercial ones do, although not all of them indicate that fact in the list of ingredients. There are good honey-sweetened mayonnaises available in natural food stores and supermarkets. Westbrae and Hollywood make excellent honey-sweetened safflower oil mayonnaise.

½ to 1 tsp. mustard—Stone-ground, Gulden's Spicy Brown, or Dijon mustard can be added to your basic dressing. The problem with any mustard I have found is that they all contain vinegar. The acetic acid in vinegar suspends salivary digestion, thereby slowing down the digestion of starches. If you are going to use mustard, make it the exception, not the rule.

Possible additions to your basic daily salad can include:

Avocado—This is a vegetable-fruit that combines well with salad vegetables. All varieties of avocado should be eaten when they are just slightly soft and not mushy. One way to use avocado is to mash it thoroughly with a fork and use it as a dressing. Avocado contains an abundance of natural oil, and some people experience discomfort after eating it in combination with other oils, such as those used in salad dressings or mayonnaise.

Cheese—If you wish to eat cheese, the best food to combine it with is salad, for salad with its high water content and abundance of digestive enzymes tends to counteract the mucousy properties of the cheese. Soft cheeses such as cottage cheese, ricotta cheese, jack cheese, Swiss cheese, and Muenster cheese contain more water than do the harder varieties such as cheddar, provolone, and Parmesan and are therefore preferable. It is also important to avoid imported, fermented cheeses, which are extremely acid in the system. Yellow cheeses should not be consumed because they are dyed. Goat's milk products are preferable to cow's milk products since the goat is more compatible in size with the human frame and the enormous amount of casein present in cow's milk (for the purpose of building those huge bones) is found to a much lesser extent in goat's milk.

Olives—If they are available, use naturally cured olives that do not have lactic acid added as a preservative. Olives are a rich source of natural oil, and adding them to your salad helps to make it more filling.

Seeds—Sunflower, sesame, pumpkin. All are rich in the vital elements and are fine added to salads *as long as they are in their raw state.* Once they have been roasted they are no longer nutritious but are extremely acid-forming in the body. Seeds can be used in small quantities since they are concentrated. One or 2 teaspoons in your daily salad is sufficient.

PORTANT NOTE: It is not recommended that you add
ocado, cheese, olives, and seeds to your salad all the
e, nor is it advisable to add all of these ingredients at
same time. They are concentrated foods and take
ger to pass through the digestive system. Use them
criminately and sparingly so that you do not turn your
nt and cleansing daily salad into a heavy, clogging meal.

KNOW HOW TO USE
OUR BASIC EVERYDAY SALAD

e Basic Everyday Salad is a good meal on its own and
important accompaniment to whatever else you may
eating. However, its most important use is as a basis for
ar main meal. From now on, try to visualize eating
als that consist of one dish or bowl—as the case may
Simply make the Basic Everyday Salad and dress it up
h whatever else you wish to eat. For example, if you
h to have rice or potatoes, add these to your salad. If
a are planning on having steamed vegetables, such as
ccoli, zucchini, carrots, string beans, or peas, add these
your salad in the quantities you desire. Macaroni can be
led to the Basic Everyday Salad, if that is what you are
ving. You can add roast beef, or chicken, or cheese.
e idea is to teach yourself to eat salad as your main
urse. What you put into the salad—along with the basic
redients—depends on what cravings you are having.
member to properly combine your additions. Do not
l meat and potatoes to the same salad! If you are
ling protein, do not add carbohydrates. Whatever you
add will pass through your system more easily be-
se, eating in this way, the bulk of your meal will always
sist of raw vegetables.

In the following pages you will find recipes for one-dish meals. The possibilities are endless. As you begin to make your main meal a salad meal, you will find combinations that are particularly satisfying to you. Do not hesitate to eat the same salad combination several days in a row if you are enjoying it and feel satisfied after eating it. The idea that your diet must consist of an enormous variety can become an idea of the past, for it is not at all commensurate with total health. Animals living in nature and even animals in captivity thrive on the same few dietary foods for their entire lives. Humans are the only ones subjecting themselves to so much variety—and, of course, they have the largest variety of diseases. Feel free to eat the same meal over and over if it pleases you—especially if it is a salad meal. You will naturally make the change to something else when your body requires that you do so.

THE BASIC EVERYDAY SALAD
with Olives and Whole Wheat Croutons

1 Basic Everyday Salad
  Basic Salad Dressing
to 1 cup sliced olives
4 slices whole wheat bread
2 Tbs. butter
2 cloves garlic

Prepare the Basic Everyday Salad. Add the basic lemon and oil dressing and the sliced olives. Cut the bread into small cubes. In a medium-sized frying pan, melt the butter. Mince the garlic and sauté it in the butter until it starts to crisp. Remove the garlic pieces. Toss in the bread cubes and sauté them, stirring constantly, until they are crispy. Sprinkle the croutons lightly with seasoned salt and add them to the salad. Toss well to blend all the ingredients.

This makes a delicious salad meal for 2 or 3 people. The bread is easily digested because of all the salad greens. Be sure that you do not combine this salad with any animal protein foods, for this will greatly slow the digestive process. For most people, olives combine compatibly with bread, and the combination in this salad is light and digestible.

THE BASIC EVERYDAY SALAD
With Meat

If you are trying to break a meat-eating habit but fin
yourself experiencing an overwhelming craving for mea
one of the best ways to deal with this craving is to put th
meat right into the basic salad. The flavors blend nicel
You end up eating less meat and more salad. The meat
more digestible accompanied by a large quantity of fres
vegetables.

Try to buy farm-raised beef if at all possible. That wa
you at least avoid the ill-effects of the dubious mas
feeding practices of the cattle industry. Perhaps with som
searching you will be able to locate a source for fres
farm-raised beef or poultry in your area.

1 Basic Everyday Salad
  Basic Salad Dressing
2 portions of whatever type of meat you are craving,
  i.e., steak or roast beef

Prepare the Basic Everyday Salad and add the dressin
Prepare the meat according to your taste and slice it thi
into bite-sized pieces. Add the meat to your salad and tos
well.

This should satisfy the meat craving and the sala
needs of 2 hungry people. Remember to consume lots
fresh carrot-celery juice the next day to neutralize the ac
effects of the meat in your system. Be sure that you do n
combine your beef salad with *any* starch (rice, potato,
bread).

THE BASIC EVERYDAY SALAD
with Chicken

Basic Everyday Salad
Basic Salad Dressing
portions of chicken
Tbs. of mayonnaise (optional)

Prepare the Basic Everyday Salad and add the dressing.
Prepare the chicken according to your taste, cut it into
bite-sized pieces, add it to the salad, stir in the mayonnaise, and serve.

This should be a satisfying meal for 2. Remember! Do
not combine your chicken salad with *any* starch.

THE HEAVY WORK SCHEDULE SALAD

This finely chopped salad is great to serve as your evening meal after a day of eating just fruit. It is filling and satisfying. You will have an enormous amount of energy for your work when you eat this way. Make a large glass of carrot-celery-spinach-lettuce juice and drink it while you prepare the salad. This salad is simply the Basic Everyday Salad with all of the ingredients finely chopped and additions of finely grated carrot and chopped olives.

1 Basic Everyday Salad
2 large carrots
1 cup green olives stuffed with pimiento
½ cup black olives
¼ cup bouquet garni
   Seasoned salt or salt-free seasoning to taste
2 Tbs. fresh-squeezed lemon juice
½ cup unrefined safflower or olive oil

Prepare the Basic Everyday Salad, finely chopping all the ingredients. Grate the carrots on the finest grater you have. I have one imported from Switzerland and made by Bircher Brenner, which grates in both directions and makes the carrot extremely soft. Quarter the green olives and cut the black ones from the seeds in small pieces. Add these to the salad. Add the bouquet garni and the seasoned salt. Whip together the oil and the lemon juice. Pour the mixture over the salad. Toss well, cover, and place in the refrigerator for approximately 15 minutes to give the flavors a chance to blend.

THE HEAVY WORK SCHEDULE SALAD
Chapatis

Chapatis are a large, soft, flat bread based on a recipe eaten by the Hunzas in northern India, one of the longest living and healthiest races of people so far discovered on earth. Garden of Eatin', 5300 Wilshire Boulevard, in Los Angeles, California, makes a truly excellent chapati from unleavened whole wheat flour, corn, barley, water, and sea salt. If you cannot get chapatis, any whole wheat flat bread or pita will do.

When you are in need of something just a little heavier than salad, rolling your salad in a chapati is a fine solution. Heat a large frying pan until a drop of water on it sizzles. Place a chapati on the pan for a few seconds. Turn it and heat the other side for a few seconds. (You cannot leave chapatis on the frying pan for too long or they become crisp and are impossible to roll.) Place a good portion of salad in the center of the chapati. Roll it like a tortilla or fold up three sides, envelope-style. The Heavy Work Schedule Salad, since it is finely chopped, works particularly well in a chapati. The combination is absolutely delicious. Chapatis are so light you can eat three or four with salad and not feel weighed down at all. Be careful not to put cheese on any salad you are rolling in chapatis, since the cheese and bread are a slow-to-digest, incompatible combination.

RAINY DAY SALAD

This salad, a combination of steamed vegetables and the Basic Everyday Salad, makes a satisfying meal. These amounts will serve 3 or 4 as a main course.

2 Tbs. unrefined safflower oil
2 cups fresh string beans, cut into 1-inch pieces
1 head cauliflower, cut in small flowerettes
2 cups sliced carrots
1 tsp. arrowroot
1 cup water
1 vegetable bouillon cube (optional)
1 tsp. oregano
1 Basic Everyday Salad, omitting the tomato
¼ tsp. thyme
  Sea salt to taste
2 tsp. fresh-squeezed lemon juice
½ cup unrefined safflower or olive oil
1 tsp. mayonnaise (optional)

In a heavy saucepan, heat the 2 Tbs. safflower oil. Add the string beans, the cauliflower, and the carrots and stir to coat with oil. Dissolve the arrowroot in the water and pour it over the vegetables. Add the vegetable bouillon and the oregano and bring to a boil. Continue stirring until the bouillon dissolves and the sauce begins to thicken slightly. Cover, reduce the heat to medium-low, and simmer 15 to 20 minutes until the vegetables are tender and the sauce is thick.

While the vegetables are cooking prepare the Basic Everyday Salad. Add the steamed vegetables, sauce included, to the salad greens. Add the thyme and sea salt. Whip together the lemon juice, oil, and mayonnaise. Pour the dressing over the salad. Toss well and serve.

ZUCCHINI RICE SALAD

This salad calls for basmati rice, which is a white, unrefined rice imported from Pakistan. If you cannot find basmati, substitute long-grain brown rice. Make an effort to use an unrefined grain, whenever possible. The salad will have more flavor and far greater nutritional benefits. This salad will serve 3 or 4 people as a main course.

        2 cups basmati rice
        4 cups water
        2 Tbs. unrefined safflower oil
        1 tsp. sea salt
6 to 8 small zucchini
        2 Tbs. unrefined safflower or olive oil
        1 tsp. oregano
     ½ cup water
        1 Basic Everyday Salad (tomatoes are optional)
        1 cup green olives stuffed with pimiento
     ½ cup unrefined safflower or olive oil
        3 tsp. fresh-squeezed lemon juice
           Pinch of thyme
           Seasoned salt or salt-free seasoning to taste

Prepare the basmati. Combine the rice, 4 cups water, 2 Tbs. safflower oil, and sea salt in a heavy saucepan. Bring to a boil. Stir gently and cover. Reduce the heat to low and simmer the rice 17 minutes. Uncover, fluff with a fork, and allow to cool slightly. *NOTE:* Do not lift the lid while cooking.

Meanwhile, prepare the zucchini. Cut each zucchini in ¼-inch slices. Heat 2 Tbs. oil in a heavy saucepan or wok. Add the zucchini and stir well to coat the vegetables with oil. Add the oregano, and ½ cup water. Bring to a boil, cover, and steam the zucchini over low heat 5 to 10 minutes or until just tender when pierced with a sharp knife. Allow to cool while you prepare the salad.

Prepare the Basic Everyday Salad. Add the basmati rice and the zucchini, and slice the olives, sprinkling them on top. Whip together the oil and lemon juice. Add the thyme to the salad. Pour the dressing over all and mix well. Season with seasoned salt to taste.

POTATO LOVER'S SALAD

This salad, as indicated by its title, is a favorite among those who are trying to break a fried potato addiction. The potatoes are made easier to digest by the presence of all the raw vegetables. This salad is a meal in itself, or it can be combined with Pea and Carrot Salad for a salad feast.

2	Tbs. unrefined safflower oil
5 to 6	red or White Rose potatoes (peeling optional), enough to yield 2 cups when diced
1	bunch broccoli
1	Basic Everyday Salad (tomatoes are optional)
1	clove garlic (optional)
	Pinch of thyme, oregano, and bouquet garni
2	Tbs. fresh-squeezed lemon juice
⅓	cup unrefined safflower or olive oil
1	Tbs. mayonnaise
	Seasoned salt or salt-free seasoning to taste

Heat the 2 tablespoons safflower oil in a large skillet. Cut the potatoes into small cubes. Toss the potatoes in the hot oil, lower the heat, and sauté the potatoes, turning them frequently until they are crusty on the outside and soft on the inside. While the potatoes are cooking, remove the heavy stems from the broccoli, separate the flowerettes, and steam them over boiling water in a vegetable steamer for 7 to 10 minutes or until the broccoli is tender when pierced with a sharp knife. Do not overcook the broccoli or allow it to be become mushy. Set the broccoli and potatoes aside to cool slightly while you prepare the salad.

Prepare the Basic Everyday Salad. If you are using garlic, cut the clove in half and rub it on the bottom of a large wooden bowl. Break the lettuce into bite-sized pieces and place it in the bowl. Coarsely chop the spinach and add it to the lettuce. Cut the tomatoes into eighths. Peel the cucumber and cut it into small chunks. Arrange the sprouts along the rim of the bowl. Place the tomatoes and cucumber in the center of the circle of sprouts. Add the warm potatoes and the broccoli. Sprinkle the herbs and seasoned salt on top. Beat the lemon juice, oil, and mayonnaise together with a fork. Pour the dressing over the salad and toss well. Serve immediately. Serves 2 to 3 potato lovers.

ROMAINE ROLL-UPS

For this salad large romaine lettuce leaves are used as wrappers. The quantities used will serve 3 people.

2 large ripe avocados
2 large ripe tomatoes
1 cucumber
  Sea salt, seasoned salt, or salt-free seasoning to taste
1 Tbs. fresh-squeezed lemon juice
1 Tbs. finely chopped red onion (optional)
1 large head romaine lettuce

Slice the avocados in half lengthwise. Remove the seeds and scoop the fruit from the skin into a medium-sized bowl. Mash it thoroughly with a fork. Coarsely chop the tomatoes, peel and chop the cucumber, and add these to the avocado. Add the salt, the lemon juice, and the chopped onion, and mix well. Wash the lettuce leaves, dry them thoroughly, and arrange the leaves around the sides of a large wooden bowl in the form of a flower. Mound the avocado mixture in the center. To eat, place a large spoonful of avocado in the center of a lettuce leaf and roll the leaf tortilla-fashion.

AVOCADO-SPROUT SALAD

1 cup lentil sprouts
2 cups mung bean sprouts
2 cups alfalfa sprouts
2 tomatoes
1 cucumber
1 scallion (optional)
1 large or 2 small avocados
1 clove garlic (optional)
2 Tbs. fresh-squeezed lemon juice
  Seasoned salt or salt-free seasoning to taste

Mix the sprouts together in a large wooden bowl. Chop the tomatoes, peel the cucumber, and cut it into cubes. Add these to the sprouts. Mince the scallion and sprinkle it on the vegetables. Scoop the avocado fruit from the skins into a small wooden bowl and mash it along with a crushed garlic clove. Beat in the lemon juice and the seasoned salt. Add the avocado to the vegetables and mix thoroughly so that all the ingredients are well combined. This is a high-energy salad (all those live sprouts!) that can be served with crisp carrot sticks and corn chips for a delicious meal for two.

SALADE NICOISE
(Diced Vegetable Salad)

        3 large carrots
7 to 8 medium-sized new potatoes (peeling optional)
        1 lb. fresh string beans
        2 cups fresh or frozen peas
        1 large bunch broccoli
        1 cup mayonnaise (homemade is preferable)
      ½ tsp. thyme
        Seasoned salt or salt-free seasoning to taste

In the top of a vegetable steamer, steam the carrots and the potatoes together whole until they are just tender when pierced with a sharp knife, approximately ½ hour. While they are steaming, prepare the other vegetables. Cut the string beans into ½-inch pieces, shell the peas, and cut the broccoli into small flowerettes. When the carrots and potatoes are tender, set them aside to cool and place the peas and string beans in the top of the vegetable steamer. Steam them together for 15 minutes (5 minutes for frozen peas, which should be added last), and then add the broccoli flowerettes and continue steaming another 10 minutes or until the broccoli is tender. While the green vegetables are steaming, cut the potatoes and carrots into small cubes. Mix all of the warm vegetables together in a large bowl. Add the mayonnaise, the thyme, and the seasoned salt. Mix well to combine all the flavors. Serve on lettuce leaves on individual plates and garnish with lots of fresh quartered tomatoes and cucumber slices or combine with the Basic Everyday Salad. Serves 4.

Variation: Approximately 1 cup of Perfect Herb Dressing can be substituted for the mayonnaise.

GRANDMA'S COLE SLAW

> 1 head cabbage
> 1 large carrot
> 1 small green pepper
> 2 scallions
>   Fresh-squeezed juice of lemon
> 1 Tbs. honey diluted in ½ cup boiling water (optional)
> 1 to 2 cups mayonnaise
>   Seasoned salt or salt-free seasoning to taste

Grate the cabbage on a medium grater or chop it to a fine consistency. Grate the carrot on a fine grater. Mince the green pepper and the scallions. Add the vegetables to the cabbage and mix well. Combine the lemon juice with the honey and boiling water and pour it over the slaw. Add enough mayonnaise for the creamy consistency you desire, and seasoned salt to taste. Stir thoroughly so that all the ingredients are well combined. This cole slaw should be refrigerated for several hours before serving. Serves 8.

GOLDEN CORN SALAD

    8 ears corn
    1 pint cherry tomatoes
    1 stalk celery
    1 cucumber
    ½ cup sliced green or black olives (optional)
½ to 1 cup mayonnaise
    ½ tsp. turmeric or curry powder
       Sea salt, seasoned salt, or salt-free seasoning to taste

Place the corn in a vegetable steamer and steam 5 to 10 minutes over boiling water. Cool slightly and cut the kernels from the cobs. Cut the cherry tomatoes into halves and set aside. Mince the celery. Peel the cucumber and cut it into thin slices. Add the celery, the cucumber slices, and the olives to the corn. Mix the mayonnaise with the turmeric or curry powder and the salt and pour it over the corn salad. Mix well. Gently stir in the tomatoes and chill before serving. Serves 4 to 6 people. This salad is a nice addition to a buffet dinner and combines well with the Basic Everyday Salad and Honey Corn Bread.

LISA'S FARMER'S CHOP SUEY

My daughter Lisa was a little dairy "freak," and she was always stuffed up and mucousy from it. This salad was the best way I found to help her indulge her dairy craving and yet minimize the ill-effects. I eliminated the radishes and scallions when I made it for her.

1 head iceberg lettuce
4 tomatoes
1 cucumber
6 radishes (optional)
1 stalk celery
2 scallions (optional)
1 cup sour cream
1 cup raw cottage cheese
   Sea salt or seasoned salt to taste (optional)

Cut the lettuce, tomatoes, and peeled cucumber into bite-sized pieces. Thinly slice the radishes and celery, and the scallions, using some of the green. Place the vegetables in a large bowl. Mix together the sour cream and the cottage cheese and pour this over the salad. Sprinkle with salt. Mix thoroughly and serve immediately.

This salad cannot stand too long because it becomes watery, so if you wish it to be cold, use all your ingredients straight out of the refrigerator. This amount serves 4. Farmer's Chop Suey is a nice accompaniment to a large bowl of Garlic String Beans. Be sure you do not use bread or any other starch with this salad. The presence of the cottage cheese (protein) makes it incompatible with starches.

CAESAR SALAD

This popular salad, containing egg yolk and Parmesan cheese, is fine combined with vegetables. It combines poorly with starches because of the heavy protein in the dressing.

    head butter, romaine, or red leaf lettuce
    bunch spinach
    clove garlic
    cup unrefined olive oil
    Fresh-squeezed juice of 1 small lemon
    egg yolk
    tsp. Dijon mustard
    cup freshly grated Parmesan cheese
    tsp. sea salt (optional)

Wash and dry the lettuce and spinach, break them into bite-sized pieces, and set them aside. In a large wooden bowl, mash the garlic clove with a fork. Add the olive oil, stir thoroughly, and remove the garlic pieces. Add the lemon juice and beat with a fork until creamy. Add the egg yolk and the mustard and continue beating. Add ¼ cup of the Parmesan cheese. Mix in the greens and toss well. Add the salt and the remaining cheese and mix well. Serves 4.

MUSHROOM AND SWISS CHEESE SALAD

When you are craving cheese, this is a good way to eat it, and you can substitute Muenster, jack, or any other (preferably soft) cheese for the Swiss. Remember not to com-

bine this salad, containing protein, with a starch. Mixed
Steamed Vegetables would be an excellent accompaniment

- 1 bunch spinach
- 1 head romaine or red leaf lettuce
- ½ lb. fresh mushrooms*
- 1 cup green or black olives
- ¼ cup minced celery
- ½ lb. Swiss cheese
- 2 Tbs. fresh-squeezed lemon juice
  Unrefined olive oil
- 1 clove garlic, pressed
- ¼ tsp. sea salt (optional)
- ½ tsp. bouquet garni
- 2 Tbs. mayonnaise

Wash and thoroughly dry the spinach and the lettuce
Chop the spinach and break the lettuce into bite-size
pieces. Wash the mushrooms briefly under cold water. (D
not overwash them or they become soggy.) Cut the mush
rooms into thin slices and add them to the greens. Ad
the olives and the celery. Slice the cheese into matchstick
sized pieces and combine it with the vegetables.

Put the lemon juice into a measuring cup and add oliv
oil to measure ⅓ cup. Add the garlic, sea salt, and bouque
garni and beat in the mayonnaise with a fork until th
dressing has a thick, creamy consistency. Remove the garli
pieces and pour the dressing over the salad and toss wel
This makes a large and delicious salad for 4 people.

*Note: If possible, select mushrooms that have no separa
tion between the cap and the stem. When they have begu
to open, they are no longer fresh.

HINESE VEGETABLE SALAD

- lb. mung bean sprouts
- lb. snow peas
- small Chinese cabbage
- scallions (optional)
- carrot
- cup soy sauce or slightly less tamari
- Tbs. brown rice vinegar*
- cup honey-sweetened ketchup
- tsp. garlic salt (or rub the bowl with fresh garlic before you place the vegetables in it)
- cup unrefined safflower oil

eam the bean sprouts and snow peas in 2 cups boiling ater until the snow peas are tender but still bright green d the bean sprouts are wilted. Drain thoroughly. Slice e Chinese cabbage very thin and toss it with the warm getables. Mince the scallions, using some of the green. rate the carrot on a fine grater and add it to the other getables. In a small bowl, blend together the soy sauce, ce vinegar, ketchup, garlic salt, and safflower oil. Pour the essing over the salad and mix well. This salad can be ten slightly warm or chilled a few hours before serving. is makes a good lunch for a change of pace and mbines well with Vegetable Egg Rolls. It is also delicious lled in hot tortillas. Serves 3 to 4.

lote: Brown rice vinegar makes a tangier salad, but you ll probably ultimately want to omit it as you eliminate ments from your diet.

BEST POTATO SALAD

2 lbs. White Rose or new potatoes
½ cup finely chopped celery
1 cup mayonnaise
1 tsp. Gulden's Spicy Brown mustard
¼ tsp. seasoned salt or salt-free seasoning
Pinch of thyme

Place the potatoes in the top of a vegetable steamer or in 2 inches of water in a heavy saucepan and steam them until they are just tender when pierced with a sharp knife, approximately 25 to 30 minutes. Allow them to cool slightly and then cut them into slices or small cubes. It is not necessary to peel the potatoes before or after steaming. The skins add texture to the salad. Peeling is optional. Add the chopped celery. Mix together the mayonnaise and the mustard. Pour the dressing over the potatoes. Add the seasoned salt and the thyme and mix well to combine all the ingredients. Serves 6. Leftover potato salad keeps well overnight.

Potato is a heavy carbohydrate, and because of the small amount of eggs in the mayonnaise, this salad does not digest quickly. Combine potato salad with a Basic Everyday Salad to expedite its digestion, and try to avoid eating it with anything heavy. *When you are eating potato salad, it should be the heaviest food at that meal.*

STRING BEAN–POTATO SALAD

This salad is lighter than regular potato salad, especially if you use lots of string beans.

1 recipe Best Potato Salad
1 lb. fresh string beans

Steam the potatoes. Cut the string beans into 1-inch pieces, and while the potatoes are cooling, steam the string beans in the vegetable steamer over boiling water for approximately 15 to 20 minutes or until they are tender when pierced with a sharp knife. Run them under cold water *briefly* to fix the color and to crisp. Combine the potatoes and the string beans and proceed as in the recipe for Best Potato Salad. Serve this salad warm or chilled. It is enough for 6 and combines well with the Basic Everyday Salad.

PEA AND POTATO SALAD

Prepare String Bean and Potato Salad, substituting 2 cups fresh shelled peas for the string beans.

PEA AND CARROT SALAD

- 6 large carrots
- 4 cups fresh shelled peas (approximately 4 lbs. in the shell) or 1 16-oz. bag frozen peas
- 1 head butter, romaine, or iceberg lettuce
- 1 cup mayonnaise (homemade mayonnaise is particularly good in this recipe)
- ¼ tsp. seasoned salt or salt-free seasoning
- ¼ tsp. thyme (optional)

Place the whole washed carrots in the top of a vegetable steamer and steam them over boiling water for approximately 20 to 25 minutes or until they are tender when pierced with a sharp knife. Remove them from the steamer and set them aside to cool. Steam the peas in the top of the steamer for 10 minutes. While they are steaming, wash and coarsely chop the lettuce leaves, and at the end of the 10 minutes place the lettuce in the steamer on top of the peas. Continue steaming another 5 to 10 minutes until the peas are tender and the lettuce is wilted. (If using frozen peas, steam together with the lettuce for 5 to 10 minutes only.) Dice the carrots. Combine them with the peas and the lettuce in a large bowl. Add the mayonnaise, seasoned salt, and thyme. Mix well and chill slightly before serving. This salad serves 3 to 4 and combines well with the Basic Everyday Salad.

NGY GREEN COLE SLAW

head cabbage
Tbs. finely chopped fresh dill
Tbs. finely chopped fresh parsley
cup sour cream
cup mayonnaise
Fresh-squeezed juice of 1 small lemon (approximately 2 Tbs.)
Sea salt to taste

ate the cabbage on a medium grater or chop it to a fine nsistency. In a bowl large enough for easy mixing, mbine the cabbage, dill, and parsley. Blend together the ır cream, mayonnaise, and lemon juice. Pour the dress- over the cabbage. Refrigerate, covered, until ready to ve. Serves 4 to 6 and combines well with Tomato Salad d a large bowl of Garlic String Beans or Steamed ›ccoli with Lemon-Butter Sauce.

YOGHURT LOVER'S SALAD NUMBER 1

If you are going to eat yoghurt, it is best to eat it with lo
of fresh vegetables to counteract its mucousy effect
your body. Be sure you do not combine a salad containir
yoghurt with any starch, since yoghurt is a heavy protei

2 cups fresh alfalfa sprouts
1 tomato, chopped
1 stalk celery, chopped
2 Tbs. finely chopped fresh parsley
1 clove garlic
1 Tbs. fresh-squeezed lemon juice
1 cup plain yoghurt (preferably the yoghurt made from goa
    milk)
    Seasoned salt, salt-free seasoning, or sea salt to taste

Combine the alfalfa sprouts with the chopped tomato ar
celery. Add the chopped parsley. In a small wooden bo
crush the garlic with a fork. Add the lemon juice ar
yoghurt and beat well. Remove the garlic pieces. Pour th
dressing over the salad, add the salt, and mix well
combine. This salad makes a good meal for 1 yoghu
lover but should not be combined with *any* starch.

YOGHURT LOVER'S SALAD NUMBER 2

2 cups fresh alfalfa sprouts
1 cup finely chopped spinach
1 small sweet red pepper, sliced
1 cucumber, peeled, quartered, and sliced
1 tomato, cut into chunks
1 clove garlic
2 Tbs. fresh-squeezed lemon juice
2 cups plain yoghurt
   Seasoned salt, salt-free seasoning, or sea salt to taste

Mix all the small vegetables together. Crush the garlic with a fork in a small wooden bowl. Add the lemon juice and yoghurt and beat well. Remove the garlic pieces. Pour the dressing over the salad, add the salt, and mix well. This salad is an ample meal for 2 yoghurt lovers. Be sure that you do *not* combine it with *any* starch.

GUACAMOLE

1 clove garlic
2 large ripe avocados
2 large ripe tomatoes
1 tsp. oregano
   Dash of cayenne pepper (optional, since cayenne is irritating
   to the sensitive linings of the digestive tract)
   Seasoned salt, salt-free seasoning, or sea salt to taste

Rub a medium-sized wooden bowl with garlic. Cut the avocados in half; remove and reserve the seeds. Scoop the fruit from the skins into the wooden bowl and mash well. Chop the tomatoes and stir into the avocado. Add the oregano, cayenne pepper, and salt. Place the avocado seeds in a deep bowl and mound the guacamole on top. The presence of the seeds keeps the guacamole from turning dark. Serve as a dip with crisp celery, corn chips, or Sokens Vegetable Chips. Serves 8.

DILLED PASTA SALAD

When you are going to eat pasta, for a pleasant change, try eating it in a salad. White flour pasta is difficult for the body to digest because of its highly refined nature. Vegetable pastas made with spinach, red pepper, beet, green onion, basil, carrot, or tomato are nice alternatives. In addition, there are an unlimited variety of Asian pastas (soba, ramen, somen, udon) made from buckwheat, brown rice, yams, and whole wheat, to mention but a few. There are also good alternatives in the Jerusalem artichoke pastas and the sesame pastas. Each of these is great, and if you are a pasta enthusiast you should try them all. Just remember the rule of thumb: The more vegetables you add to your pasta, the easier it will be to digest.

      1 lb. pasta (rotelle, fusilli, shells, elbows, or any
         combination)
      2 Tbs. finely chopped parsley
    ½ cup finely diced celery
  1½ cups chopped tomatoes
      2 cups asparagus tips, lightly seasoned
      1 clove garlic, crushed
¼ to ⅓ cup unrefined olive oil
      2 Tbs. chopped fresh dill
      2 Tbs. chopped fresh basil
         Seasoned salt or salt-free seasoning to taste

Cook the pasta according to the instructions on the package or approximately 10 minutes for al dente. Drain it in a colander. Run it under cold water and drain thoroughly. Combine the parsley, celery, tomatoes, and asparagus tips in a large bowl. Gently stir in the pasta. In a small bowl, mix together the garlic and olive oil. Add the fresh dill and basil and mix well. Remove the garlic pieces and pour the dressing over the salad. Season with salt. Mix well to combine all the ingredients. Chill and serve to 3 or 4 pasta lovers.

TOMATO SALAD

This salad is best when tomatoes are in season. It tastes particularly good in hot weather, especially if you chill it before serving. This salad combines well with potato salad, Pea and Carrot Salad, cole slaw, and any steamed vegetable.

    4 large, ripe, juicy beefsteak or Mason tomatoes
    2 Tbs. finely chopped fresh basil
    2 Tbs. fresh-squeezed lemon juice
      Unrefined olive oil
    1 clove garlic
    1 tsp. Dijon mustard
    ½ tsp. bouquet garni
      Pinch of thyme
      Sea salt to taste

Wash and dry the tomatoes, cut them into thin slices, and place them in a large glass bowl. Sprinkle the basil over the tomatoes. Put the lemon juice into a measuring cup. Add enough olive oil to measure ⅓ cup. Cut the garlic into two or three pieces and add it to the lemon and oil mixture. Add the mustard and whip the dressing with a fork. Remove the garlic pieces. Sprinkle the bouquet garni and the thyme over the sliced tomatoes. Add the sea salt. Pour the dressing over the salad and mix well. Serves 2 to 3 people.

THE TOTALLY HEALTHY PERSON SALAD

This live meal leaves you feeling so clean and energetic, you may want to eat it several times a week when good avocados are available. This is a satisfying salad for those who are trying to cut down on condiments.

  2 cups shredded lettuce
  1 cup shredded spinach
  1 medium tomato, cut into chunks
½ cup lentil sprouts
  1 large handful mung bean sprouts
  1 large handful alfalfa or red clover sprouts
  2 Tbs. finely grated carrot
½ avocado, cut into chunks
½ avocado, mashed
¼ cup fresh carrot juice

Combine all the ingredients in the order given. Serves 1 *totally healthy person*.

SALAD DRESSINGS

A few reminders: Always use fresh lemon juice when you are putting together a salad dressing. Avoid the use of vinegar whenever possible. The acetic acid in vinegar totally suspends salivary digestion, and vinegar, a ferment, causes fermentation in the system. (Your body cannot benefit nutritionally from that which is fermented.) Try to use unrefined oils in your dressings. If you are going to add mayonnaise or ketchup to any of the dressings, take advantage of the excellent sugar-free, honey-sweetened preparations available in natural foods stores.

CREAMY FRENCH DRESSING

2 Tbs. fresh-squeezed lemon juice
  Unrefined olive or safflower oil
1 clove garlic
½ tsp. bouquet garni
¼ tsp. seasoned salt or salt-free seasoning
2 Tbs. mayonnaise

Put the lemon juice into a measuring cup and add enough oil to measure ½ cup. Cut the garlic in half, place both halves on the end of a fork, and use the fork to mix the lemon juice and oil. Add the bouquet garni and seasoned salt. With the same fork, beat in the mayonnaise until the dressing has a thick, creamy consistency.

This recipe yields enough for a salad for 3 to 4 people.

CHINESE SALAD DRESSING

¼ cup soy sauce or slightly less tamari
2 Tbs. fresh-squeezed lemon juice, or 2 Tbs. brown rice vinegar
    (optional)
¼ cup honey-sweetened ketchup
½ tsp. garlic salt or 1 clove fresh garlic, crushed
¼ cup unrefined sesame or safflower oil
1 tsp. roasted sesame oil

Blend all the ingredients together and use as a dressing for Chinese Vegetable Salad or as a sauce for stir-fried vegetables. Yields approximately ⅔ cup.

ITALIAN SALAD DRESSING

3 Tbs. fresh-squeezed lemon juice
½ cup unrefined olive oil
1 tsp. dried oregano
    Pinch of thyme
½ tsp. seasoned salt or salt-free seasoning
1 clove garlic, crushed

Shake all of the ingredients in a jar with a lid. Refrigerate several hours before using so that the flavors blend and the oregano flavor is dominant. Yields approximately ⅔ cup.

Note: If you do not wish to consume garlic—which leads you to heavier foods—simply cut the garlic clove into pieces and let them sit in the dressing, removing them right before you are ready to pour the dressing over the salad.

CREAMY AVOCADO DRESSING

    1 ripe avocado
 ¼ cup mayonnaise (optional, since some people find the com-
         bination of avocado and any other oil difficult to digest)
    1 Tbs. fresh-squeezed lemon juice
    1 clove garlic, pressed (optional)
 ½ tsp. seasoned salt or salt-free seasoning
    1 tomato, finely chopped

Scoop the avocado fruit from the skin into a wooden bowl
and mash with a fork. Add the mayonnaise, lemon juice,
and garlic. Add the seasoned salt and stir in the tomato.
For an extremely smooth, creamy dressing, mix all of the
ingredients in a blender. Yields approximately 1 cup.

CAESAR DRESSING

          1 clove garlic
 ⅓ to ½ cup unrefined olive, safflower, or sunflower seed oil
    2 to 3 Tbs. fresh-squeezed lemon juice
          1 egg yolk
          1 tsp. Dijon mustard
       ½ tsp. sea salt, seasoned salt, or salt-free seasoning
             Freshly ground pepper to taste (optional)
       ½ cup freshly grated Parmesan cheese

In the bowl in which you are planning to serve the salad,
mash the garlic clove with a fork. Add the oil, stir thoroughly,
and remove the garlic pieces. Add the lemon juice and
beat with a fork until creamy. Add the egg yolk, mustard,
salt, and pepper. Mix well. Add ¼ cup of the cheese.
Reserve the remaining cheese to add to the greens before
tossing. Yields approximately ¾ cup.

TAMARI SALAD DRESSING

- 1 clove garlic
- ¼ cup unrefined safflower oil
- 2 Tbs. fresh-squeezed lemon juice
- 1 Tbs. tamari
- ¼ cup mayonnaise

Cut the garlic in half and rub the salad bowl with the two cut pieces. Combine the remaining ingredients and mix thoroughly. Yields approximately ⅔ cup.

MUSTARD CREAM SALAD DRESSING

When you are craving a creamy dressing, this one is a good alternative to those requiring mayonnaise or cheese.

- 2 Tbs. fresh-squeezed lemon juice
- ¼ cup unrefined olive or safflower oil
- ½ tsp. thyme
- ¼ tsp. oregano
- 1 Tbs. Gulden's Spicy Brown mustard
- ½ cup sour cream

Whip together the lemon juice and the olive oil. Pour them over the salad. Add the herbs and toss well. Whip together the mustard and the sour cream. Pour them over the salad. Toss again to blend flavors. Yields enough for 1 large salad.

PERFECT HERB DRESSING

 2 Tbs. fresh-squeezed lemon juice
½ cup unrefined olive or safflower oil
 1 clove garlic
½ tsp. bouquet garni
½ tsp. thyme
½ tsp. oregano
½ tsp. basil
½ tsp. sea salt, seasoned salt, or salt-free seasoning

Place the lemon juice and the oil in a jar with a tight-fitting lid. Depending on how much garlic you wish to eat, crush the clove of garlic or simply cut it in half and add it to the oil-lemon mixture. Measure in the herbs and the salt. Cover the jar tightly and shake the dressing until it thickens slightly and all the ingredients are well combined. Discard the large garlic pieces. This piquant dressing is enough for 1 large salad.

REAL FRENCH DRESSING

    1 clove garlic
    ⅓ cup unrefined olive oil
    2 Tbs. fresh-squeezed lemon juice
    1 tsp. Dijon mustard
    ½ tsp. bouquet garni
       Pinch of thyme
    ¼ tsp. seasoned salt or salt-free seasoning

Mash the garlic clove with a fork in a large wooden bowl. Add the oil, stir well, and remove the garlic pieces. Add the lemon juice and whip with a fork until creamy. Add the mustard, bouquet garni, thyme, and seasoned salt. Mix well. Pile the salad greens on top. Toss and serve. Yields approximately ½ cup.

THOUSAND ISLAND DRESSING

    ½ cup mayonnaise
    2 Tbs. honey-sweetened ketchup
    1 Tbs. fresh-squeezed lemon juice
    ½ cup finely chopped or grated cucumber, or 1 finely chopped
       dill pickle
    ¼ tsp. seasoned salt or salt-free seasoning

Stir together the mayonnaise and ketchup. Add the lemon juice, the chopped cucumber or pickle, and the seasoned salt, and mix well. This yields enough for 1 large salad.

MONSIEUR DUCELLIER'S HOMEMADE MAYONNAISE

When I was a college student, I spent one summer on an exchange program in Avignon, France. I lived with a wonderful French family by the name of Ducellier. Monsieur Ducellier's hobby was fine cooking, and one afternoon, sitting in his kitchen, I learned the art of making homemade mayonnaise. This is a labor of love. The process can take nearly an hour to complete, from start to finish. Making mayonnaise by hand is a slow meditation, and the results are extremely rewarding. In addition to its superior taste, homemade mayonnaise does not contain sweeteners, and salt can be omitted.

To make mayonnaise by hand successfully, you must have all your ingredients at room temperature and you must use a glass or ceramic bowl for mixing. Metal will not work.

> 2 egg yolks
> 1 tsp. Dijon mustard
> 2 Tbs. fresh-squeezed lemon juice
> ½ tsp. sea salt
> 1 to 2 cups unrefined safflower oil

In a small bowl, combine the egg yolks, mustard, lemon juice, and salt. Mix well. Place the bowl on a towel so that it will not travel as you mix. Drizzle the oil, *drop by drop,* into the bowl, stirring constantly with a teaspoon. The stirring action should come from the wrist in an easy rhythm. Continue drizzling in the oil until the mayonnaise suddenly turns thick. This will not happen before you have added at least 1 cup of oil. There will be a sudden change in consistency. The mayonnaise will become thicker and lighter. When the color is pale yellow and the thickness is such that the teaspoon can almost stand up by itself, the process is complete. This should require almost an hour of stirring and nearly all of the oil. Cover the mayonnaise tightly and refrigerate it until you are ready to use it.

Homemade mayonnaise is special. You can serve it as a sauce for steamed broccoli or Brussels sprouts. It is especially good substituted for bottled mayonnaise on Pea and Carrot Salad or Salade Nicoise. It is delicious added to salad dressings or on beefsteak tomato sandwiches. This recipe yields approximately 1½ to 2 cups.

EASY BLENDER MAYONNAISE

This recipe yields a product *almost* as good as the home-made mayonnaise and takes far less time. Be careful not to overblend the ingredients. Overblending causes the mayonnaise to separate. Have all the ingredients at room temperature.

   2 egg yolks
 ½ tsp. dry mustard
   2 Tbs. fresh-squeezed lemon juice
 ¼ tsp. sea salt
   1 cup unrefined safflower oil

Put the egg yolks, dry mustard, 1 Tbs. of the lemon juice, salt, and ¼ cup of the safflower oil into the blender. Blend until these ingredients are combined, approximately 10 seconds. Add the rest of the oil, in a steady fine stream, blending all the while. Blend just until the mayonnaise thickens and no longer. Add the second tablespoon of lemon juice. Blend a few seconds more and refrigerate. Yields approximately 1¼ cups.

4

SOUPS AND SANDWICHES

Homemade, Wholesome, and Nourishing

In soups and sandwiches, use fresh ingredients. Use fresh butter, unrefined oils, fresh vegetables, and seasonings without chemical additives. The best sandwich is properly combined. Do not use protein foods as sandwich fillings. On fresh whole grain or flourless bread, add the vegetable or vegetable-fruit ingredients that will facilitate digestion.

TRANSITION DIET MEALS

The optimum diet for health, proper weight control, and vitality relies heavily on fresh fruits and vegetables. But with all the food addictions (habits) that most of us have developed, it can take some time to become totally comfortable with that diet.

It is best in most cases to move away from your addictions *slowly*. In this way you avoid feelings of tension or deprivation. You can systematically eliminate one or two foods at a time, as you feel that your body no longer needs them. Move at your own speed and be your own judge. For example, you may be able to eliminate sugar, then coffee, then meat or alcohol, or you may be able to eliminate some or all of these at once. If you are experiencing tension, a dissatisfied feeling after eating, or preoccupations with cravings, you are probably moving too fast.

I have known people who have abruptly given up all junk food, red meat, dairy products, alcohol, and coffee. They immediately experienced a new exhilaration and lightness and could not even be tempted to revert to old eating habits. Others have had to move more slowly, giving up cigarettes, then sugar, then meat, and so on down the line. The important point is the direction. If you are always going in the direction of the optimum diet, eating as many fruit and salad meals as you can, while still maintaining a relaxed feeling, you are doing what is best *for you*.

The transition diet meals help you to move to a level of healthier eating. They are heavier than fruit or salad, but lighter than what you have been accustomed to in most cases. Transition diets are designed to be heavy enough so that you feel satisfied after eating, and they are always properly combined.

SOUPS AND SANDWICHES

Fresh homemade soups are especially useful in your transition diet during cooler weather. Use fresh ingredients whenever possible. Use fresh butter, unrefined oils, vegetables in season, and vegetable bouillons that are salt free and devoid of chemicals. Excellent vegetable bouillons are available at natural foods stores. On all occasions avoid the use of beef or chicken bouillons, which are extremely acid-forming in the system. Combined with a salad or a sandwich, vegetable soups make a soothing and satisfying meal.

SOUPS

DAIRYLESS CORN CHOWDER

   Eight ears fresh corn
1 stalk celery
1 small onion
2 Tbs. unrefined safflower oil
6 cups water
1 Tbs. cornstarch or arrowroot
¼ cup cold water
½ tsp. sea salt, seasoned salt, or salt-free seasoning
1 vegetable bouillon cube
¼ tsp. ground coriander

Cut the kernels from the ears of corn. (In selecting corn, choose ears on which the kernels are in regular rows rather than unevenly spaced.) Coarsely chop the celery and onion. In a medium-sized heavy saucepan, heat the safflower oil. Add the celery and onion and sauté until they are soft, stirring frequently. Add the kernels of corn, mix well to coat with oil, and sauté briefly. Add the water and bring to a boil. While the soup is coming to a boil, dissolve the cornstarch or arrowroot in the cold water. Add this thickener to the soup, with the salt, bouillon, and coriander. Bring to a boil, stirring constantly, reduce the heat, and simmer the soup 15 to 20 minutes. Allow the soup to cool slightly, place 4 cups in the blender, and blend on a high speed until smooth. Strain through a medium sieve. Return the puree to the soup pot, adjust the seasonings, reheat the chowder just to the boiling point, and serve. This recipe is enough for 2 to 3 people. Use the chowder as the main part of your meal and accompany it with a large salad, without cheese, and Crusty Garlic Toast.

CARROT BISQUE

2 Tbs. unrefined safflower oil
1 small onion
1 stalk celery
5 cups carrots, cut in ⅛-inch rounds
4 cups water
1 vegetable bouillon cube
½ tsp. bouquet garni
½ tsp. basil
1 Tbs. fresh butter
Seasoned salt or salt-free seasoning to taste

Heat the oil in a medium-sized soup pot. Chop the onion, slice the celery, and add them to the oil. Sauté them for several minutes, stirring occasionally, until the onion begins to soften. Add the carrot rounds to the sautéing vegetables. Mix well to coat them with oil. Add the water and bring the soup to a boil. Add the vegetable bouillon and the herbs. Reduce the heat to medium-low and simmer, covered, for 10 to 15 minutes or until the carrots are tender. Remove 1½ cups of the sliced carrots from the soup and set them aside. Strain the remaining soup and blend the vegetables into a puree in a blender, reserving the remaining broth. Recombine the carrots, the puree, and the broth. Stir well and bring the bisque gently to a boil. Add the butter and seasoned salt to taste. Serves 3 to 4. Small children love this carrot bisque.

EASY VEGETABLE NOODLE SOUP

- 8 cups water
- 1 medium onion, coarsely chopped
- 4 scallions, sliced
- 1 clove garlic, minced (optional)
- 1 large stalk celery, sliced
- 3 medium carrots, cut into ¼-inch rounds
- 1 cup fresh or frozen peas
- 2 medium zucchini, cut into ¼-inch rounds
- ½ head small cabbage, cut into bite-sized chunks (3 to 4 cups)
- 1 tsp. thyme
- 2 tsp. oregano
- 1 tsp. basil
- 2 vegetable bouillon cubes, or 2 Tbs. white miso
- ½ tsp. sea salt (optional)
- 1 tsp. seasoned salt or salt-free seasoning (optional)
  Freshly ground pepper to taste
- 1 cup dry pasta (Vegeroni, ribbons, or whole wheat spaghetti), broken into 3-inch lengths

Bring the water to a boil in a large soup pot. Add the onion, scallions, garlic, celery, carrots, peas, zucchini, and cabbage. Return to a boil and add the thyme, oregano, basil, bouillon or miso, sea salt, seasoned salt, and pepper. Cover and simmer over medium-low heat for 15 minutes or until all the vegetables are tender.

While the soup is cooking, bring 1 qt. water to a boil in a separate saucepan. Add ½ tsp. salt and the pasta. Cook according to package directions for the pasta or until it is just al dente, not too soft. Drain well. Stir into the soup. Simmer briefly, stirring, to combine all the ingredients. Adjust the seasonings. Serve 6.

Note: Vegeroni is a vegetable pasta that is excellent and available in most supermarkets. *Kids love this soup!*

EASY MINESTRONE

- 8 cups water
- 3 medium carrots, cut into ⅛-inch rounds
- 2 stalks celery, sliced
- 4 green onions, sliced
- 1 clove garlic, minced
- 1 medium onion, sliced
- 3 cups coarsely chopped Swiss chard or bok choy greens
- 2 cups coarsely chopped cabbage
- 1 cup frozen peas
- 3 medium zucchini, cut into ¼-inch rounds, or 1 cup frozen corn
- 1 10 oz. package Fordhook lima beans
- 1 tsp. sea salt
- 2 Tbs. white or red miso, or 2 vegetable bouillon cubes
- ¼ cup chopped fresh basil, or 2 tsp. dried
- ¼ cup chopped fresh dill, or 2 tsp. dried
- ½ tsp. dried oregano
  Freshly ground black pepper to taste
- 1 cup Vegeroni or any whole wheat, sesame, or vegetable macaroni
- 2 Tbs. chopped fresh parsley
- 1 medium tomato, cut into ½-inch cubes (optional)

Bring the water to a boil in a large soup pot. Add the carrots, celery, green onions, garlic, onion, chard or bok choy, cabbage, peas, zucchini or corn, limas, salt, miso or bouillon, basil, dill, oregano, and pepper. Return to a boil and simmer, covered, for 15 minutes.

While the soup is simmering, bring 1 qt. water to a boil

in a separate saucepan. Add ½ tsp. salt and the macaroni. Cook according to package directions, until the macaroni is just al dente. Drain well and add to the soup. Stir in the chopped parsley. Before serving, add the tomato, if desired, but do not reheat. Tomato becomes very acid when cooked, so if using tomato, serve the soup warm, rather than hot, and add the tomato at the very last minute. Serves 6.

CREAM OF BROCCOLI
(Without the Cream)

    3 Tbs. unrefined safflower oil
    1 clove garlic (optional)
    1 onion
    2 stalks celery
    2 bunches broccoli
    6 cups water
    2 vegetable bouillon cubes
    ½ tsp. seasoned salt or salt-free seasoning
    ¼ tsp. thyme
    ¼ tsp. bouquet garni
    1 Tbs. butter (optional)

Heat the oil over medium-low heat in a large, heavy soup pot. Mince the garlic and add it to the oil. Chop the onion and the celery and add them to the oil. Stir and sauté gently over low heat so the vegetables soften but do not brown. Remove the heavy stalks of the broccoli and chop the rest, preserving the shape of the small flowerettes. Add the broccoli to the other vegetables and stir well to coat thoroughly with oil. Add the water and bring the soup to a boil. Add the vegetable bouillon and the seasonings. Stir until the bouillon is dissolved, reduce the heat to medium-low, and simmer the soup, covered, for 20 minutes. Cool the soup slightly and remove 2 cups of the flowerettes. Place the remaining vegetables and some of the stock in the blender. Blend at a high speed until smooth. Return the puree to the remaining broth in the pot. Add the reserved flowerettes and mix well. Bring the soup to a gentle, rolling boil. Add the butter and stir until it melts. Serves 3 or 4.

CREAMLESS CREAM OF CAULIFLOWER SOUP

Use the same ingredients and procedure as for Cream of Broccoli Soup, substituting 2 heads of cauliflower for the broccoli.

FRESH PEA SOUP

- 4 cups freshly shelled peas (approximately 4 lbs. in the shell), or 1 16-oz. bag frozen peas
- 1 head romaine or butter lettuce
- 3 Tbs. unrefined safflower oil
- 1 clove garlic (optional)
- 1 onion
- 2 stalks celery
- 6 cups water
- 2 vegetable bouillon cubes
- ½ tsp. seasoned salt or salt-free seasoning to taste
- ¼ tsp. bouquet garni
- ½ tsp. basil
- 1 Tbs. butter (optional)

Shell the peas and coarsely chop the lettuce. Heat the oil over medium-low heat in a large soup pot. Mince the garlic and add it to the oil and sauté gently. Chop the onion and celery and add them to the pot. Sauté, stirring frequently, until the vegetables are soft. Add the peas and lettuce and mix thoroughly to coat with oil. Add the water and bring the soup to a boil. Add the seasonings, stir well, and reduce the heat to medium-low. Simmer, covered, for 15 to 20 minutes or until the peas are tender. Remove 1 cup of peas from the soup, cool the rest slightly, and blend the remaining vegetables with some of the broth in a blender at high speed. Return the puree to the remaining soup, add the reserved peas, and bring the soup to a gentle boil. Add the butter and stir until it melts. Correct the seasonings. This soup can be garnished with whole wheat croutons. It combines well with Grandma's Cole Slaw and Tomato Salad. Serves 4.

GREG'S FAVORITE LENTIL SOUP

2 Tbs. unrefined safflower oil
2 cloves garlic
1 onion
2 large carrots
2 stalks celery
1½ cups lentils
7½ cups water
1 vegetable bouillon cube
Pinch of thyme
Dash of paprika
½ cup honey-sweetened ketchup (optional)
Seasoned salt or salt-free seasoning to taste

Heat the oil in a heavy soup pot. Mince the garlic, slice the onion, and sauté them in the oil, stirring frequently, until they begin to soften. Coarsely chop the carrots and the celery and add them to the oil, stirring well to coat them. Add the lentils and stir. Add the water. Bring the soup to a boil, and when it is boiling add the bouillon, thyme, and paprika. Reduce the heat to medium-low and simmer the soup, covered, for 45 minutes to 1 hour. The lentils should be extremely soft. Allow the soup to cool slightly and for a creamier consistency, puree about half of the soup in the blender. Return the puree to the pot. Stir in the ketchup and the seasoned salt. Reheat and serve. Serves 4.

SPLIT PEA SOUP

- 2 Tbs. unrefined safflower oil or 2 Tbs. fresh butter
- 1 onion
- 2 carrots
- 2 stalks celery
- 2 cups split peas
- 10 cups water
- 1 vegetable bouillon cube
- 1 Tbs. fresh butter, softened
- 1 Tbs. whole wheat pastry flour
  Seasoned salt or salt-free seasoning to taste

Heat the oil or melt the 2 Tbs. butter in a large, heavy soup pot. Chop the onion, carrots, and celery and sauté them, stirring frequently, until the onion starts to soften. Add the split peas and mix well. Add the water and bring the soup to a boil. Add the vegetable bouillon and stir the soup until it dissolves. Simmer the soup, covered, over medium-low heat, 1 hour and 10 minutes or until the split peas are extremely soft and the soup is smooth. To bind the soup so that it will not separate, mix the 1 Tbs. butter and the flour together to make a paste. Add this binder to the soup and stir well until it has dissolved. Season with seasoned salt.

This soup is always such a favorite in my family that I usually make a large quantity. It keeps well overnight. If you do not wish to make such a large quantity, the amounts given can be cut in half. This recipe makes enough soup for 4 to 5 people as a main course. Use the soup as the main course of the meal and accompany it with a large salad.

MUSHROOM AND BARLEY SOUP

   2 Tbs. unrefined safflower oil
   1 onion
   1 carrot
   1 stalk celery
 ½ lb. fresh mushrooms
   1 cup barley
   8 cups water (use 6 cups if you want a thicker soup)
   2 Tbs. tamari
   1 Tbs. fresh butter
   1 Tbs. fresh-squeezed lemon juice
   1 Tbs. minced parsley
      Seasoned salt, salt-free seasoning, or sea salt to taste

Heat the oil in a large soup pot. Finely chop the onion, carrot, and celery and add them to the oil. Sauté, stirring frequently, until the onion begins to soften. Wash the mushrooms briefly under cold water. Set aside approximately half and finely chop the other half. Add the chopped mushrooms to the sautéing vegetables and stir well to coat them with the oil. Sauté briefly, stirring constantly. Add the barley and mix well. Add the water and the tamari. Bring the soup to a boil, cover, and simmer it over medium-low heat for 1 hour and 15 minutes. While the soup simmers, melt the butter in a medium-sized frying pan. Slice the remaining mushrooms and sauté them lightly in the butter. Do not overcook them. They are ready when they are only slightly wilted. Sprinkle the mushrooms with lemon juice and parsley and set them aside.

When the soup is ready, add the sautéed mushrooms or sprinkle them over separate bowls of soup as a garnish. Taste the soup before adding sea salt or seasoned salt. It may be salty enough because of the tamari. This recipe serves 4 people.

SANDWICHES

One of the best accompaniments to soup is a sandwich. However, sandwiches as they are traditionally consumed in the American diet present a real food-combining problem. The very nature of the sandwich dictates that you start with a heavy starch (bread), which combines poorly with the traditional protein fillings (meats, cheese, poultry, fish, nut butters). Any time a protein and a starch are eaten in conjunction with one another, the result is a radical slowing of the digestive process and fermentation and putrefaction in the system. When eaten simultaneously, starches ferment and proteins putrefy. As you strive toward good health, this situation is always to be avoided.

The best sandwich, therefore, is one that combines bread with foods that will not retard the digestive action: various fresh vegetable-fruits or vegetables, such as tomatoes, sprouts, cucumbers, lettuce, or finely grated carrots. The addition of avocado to the sandwich works well for some people and not so well for others, since avocado is a fairly concentrated food. It is fine to experiment with various sandwich combinations and see which ones work best for you. Just remember that you need as much water food as possible in your diet. Since bread cannot be considered a water food, try to combine it with high-water-content fillings whenever possible.

TOMATO SANDWICH

  2 slices whole grain or flourless bread
  1 large, ripe tomato
 ½ avocado, or mayonnaise, or fresh butter
     Alfalfa sprouts
     Lettuce (optional)

The secret of making this delicious sandwich is to have good, thick slices of tomato. You can use the whole tomato on one sandwich, if you like thick sandwiches. You can use mashed avocado, mayonnaise, or butter as your spread. Or, since the tomato is so juicy, some people find that no spread at all is needed. Toast the bread lightly. *Always toast any bread you are eating to make it less mucus-forming.* Add the spread of your choice and thick slices of tomato. Add alfalfa sprouts and lettuce, if desired. If you like tomatoes, this sandwich will definitely become one of your favorite meals.

Note: Oasis, in Escondido, California, now makes a bread out of ground wheat or rye sprouts, honey, water, sea salt, and yeast. It contains no flour whatsoever and is lighter than ordinary breads. It is not irritating to those with a wheat sensitivity. Look for it at your local natural foods store.

CUCUMBER SANDWICH

2 slices whole grain or flourless bread
  Mayonnaise or fresh butter
1 cucumber
  Seasoned salt or salt-free seasoning to taste (optional)
  Alfalfa sprouts
  Lettuce (optional)

Lightly toast the bread. Use mayonnaise or butter as your spread. Peel the cucumber and thin-slice as much as you desire onto your sandwich. Add the seasoned salt, sprouts, and lettuce, if desired. Cucumber makes a terrific sandwich and does not leave you with a heavy feeling, as do meat or cheese sandwiches. You will feel satisfied but not full.

AVOCADO SANDWICH

2 slices whole grain or flourless bread
  Mayonnaise or fresh butter, if desired
½ large, ripe avocado
  Tomato slices
  Alfalfa sprouts
  Lettuce (optional)
  Seasoned salt or salt-free seasoning to taste

Some people adore avocado sandwiches. Others find them hard to digest. For some, avocado, although it is classified as a vegetable-fruit, is too concentrated and heavy to combine well with bread. You can try this sandwich and see how it feels to you.

Toast the bread lightly. Use mayonnaise or butter as a spread, if you desire, or mash the avocado with a fork and spread it on the bread. If you are not mashing the avocado, simply slice it and arrange the slices on the bread. Add tomato slices, alfalfa sprouts, and lettuce, if desired. In this case, the tomato and sprouts are essential to aid in the digestion of the sandwich. Add seasoned salt, if desired.

PITA BREAD SANDWICHES

Pita bread, which is quite popular nowadays, is a good substitute for regular bread. Use whole wheat pita bread and, if desired, warm it briefly in the oven. Do not toast it because then it is impossible to stuff. When the bread is slightly warm and pliable, cut off a thin piece along the top and stuff in the filling.

Any salad that you make can be an excellent stuffing for a pita bread sandwich, as long as the salad does not contain a heavy protein such as meat or cheese. If you do include these in your pita bread sandwich, be aware that you are making a heavy meal out of something that could be quite light and still satisfying.

RAW DEAL PITA BREAD SALAD SANDWICH

In 1977 we made and sold these out of the back of a little health foods store on the beach in Venice, California. They were extremely popular.

>   Several leaves of lettuce
>   Several leaves of spinach
>   1   tomato
>   Celery
>   Cucumber
>   1   carrot
>   ½   avocado
>   Squeeze of fresh lemon juice
>   Mayonnaise (optional)
>   1   Tbs. unrefined olive oil or safflower oil
>   2   pita pockets
>   Seasoned salt or salt-free seasoning to taste

Finely chop the lettuce, spinach, tomato, celery, and cucumber, and combine these in a small bowl. Finely grate the carrot separately. Mash the avocado separately. Add the lemon juice, oil, and seasoned salt to the salad ingredients. Add mayonnaise, if desired. Warm the pita pockets lightly, cut off the top, and spoon in a layer of avocado. Add some grated carrot and some salad. Add another layer of avocado, carrot, and salad. Top with any avocado that may be left.

Any raw vegetables you wish to eat may be included in your pita bread sandwich. Raw mushrooms, grated red cabbage, and finely chopped raw cauliflower are among the many possibilities. If you are serving a crowd, a large salad bowl with all your favorite raw vegetables combined in a salad and warm pita pockets make a wonderful meal.

The Basic Everyday Salad, the Heavy Work Schedule Salad, the Rainy Day Salad, and the Avocado-Sprout Salad are but a few of the salads that would work well stuffed into pita pockets. (See Vegetable Salads.)

5

VEGETABLE DISHES AND GRAINS

Essential Foods on the Transition Diet

After fruit and raw vegetables, the highest-water-content foods you can eat are cooked vegetables. Take advantage of all the varieties available and do not overcook or you will lose the vital nutritional elements. Whole, unprocessed grains supply nourishing building material for growing children and adults who wish to revitalize their bodies. Combine grains exclusively with high-water-content vegetables and never with concentrated proteins.

SIMPLE VEGETABLES
AND GRAINS

After fruit and raw vegetable salads, the most important ingredient in your diet is the cooked (steamed, sautéed, baked, or broiled) vegetable. Since the heat of cooking destroys many of the nutritional elements in the vegetable, however, it is essential that it be cooked correctly, which means *not overcooked!*

In this country we tend to eat our vegetables cooked to the mushy stage, which leaves them devoid of nutritional benefits. And we tend to use many canned or frozen vegetables, for the sake of convenience, when perfectly good fresh vegetables are available. Try not to cheat yourself by indulging in this self-defeating practice. Buy fresh vegetables, as locally grown as possible, whenever the opportunity arises. They are an essential water food, being comprised mostly of water (like you), and during the fall and winter months, in particular, they will probably be the mainstay of your diet.

Be adventurous when you are buying vegetables. Try all of the many varieties that are available. Try asparagus, broccoli, peas, carrots, beets, string beans, waxed beans, zucchini, summer squash, yellow squash, artichokes, mushrooms, cauliflower, new potatoes, Idaho potatoes, White Rose potatoes, sweet potatoes, yams, spaghetti squash, acorn squash, dumpling squash, banana squash, Brussels sprouts, corn, snow peas, mung bean sprouts, bok choy, Chinese cabbage—to name just a few.

One important utensil to be used in vegetable cooking is the vegetable steamer tray. The steamer tray keeps the vegetables suspended above the water while they cook and prevents them from becoming water-logged. In addition, it prevents vital nutrients from being boiled away in the water. Steamer trays are a good investment. They cost about $4.00 at most natural foods stores or kitchen specialty shops.

Although tomatoes, green peppers, eggplant, and cucumbers are popularly labeled as vegetables, they are in reality fruits. We classify as a fruit anything that has a seed, but for clarity we shall call the above vegetable-fruits. In this cookbook you will notice that there are no recipes for cooked tomatoes, eggplants, or green peppers. These are extraordinarily acid-forming in their cooked state. The cooked tomato is responsible for ulcerations in the digestive tract. When you are changing your diet you will find that one of the hardest addictions to break is the addiction to Southern Italian food, which so frequently depends on cooked tomatoes to say nothing of white flour pastas and cheeses in wrong combinations. We all at one time or another have loved this kind of food, but in the interest of health, hold on to your fond memory of eating it and try in the future to give it up. Squash and pumpkin are also vegetable-fruits. These are not harmful when cooked. Spinach, which contains a great deal of oxalic acid, which binds calcium, should also not be eaten cooked.

When you are preparing vegetables, think of them as the main dish, rather than as a side dish. Prepare a large quantity and pass individual bowls (you can use large wooden ones) that can be filled to the brim with piping hot buttery vegetables. Until you have tried this type of meal, you cannot appreciate how delicious and utterly satisfying it can be. If more courses are required, add a salad. If more than that is needed, add steamed brown rice, or basmati rice, or slices of hot buttered whole wheat toast. This type of healthy, nourishing meal will leave you feeling just great!

STEAMED BROCCOLI WITH LEMON-BUTTER SAUCE

2 bunches fresh broccoli
¼ cup fresh butter
2 Tbs. fresh-squeezed lemon juice
   Sea salt, seasoned salt, or salt-free seasoning to taste

Cut the heavy ends of the stalks from the broccoli, leaving the flower and 2 to 3 inches of the stem. Cut each stalk into individual flowerettes. Place the broccoli on a steamer tray over boiling water. Steam, covered, until the aroma permeates the air, approximately 7 to 10 minutes. The broccoli should be tender when pierced with the point of a sharp knife, and it should retain its bright color.

In a small saucepan, melt the butter over low heat. When the butter has melted, add the lemon and the seasoned salt. Pour the sauce over the hot broccoli. This amount of broccoli serves 3 to 4 people and can serve either as the main course, accompanied by a salad, or as a complement to steamed brown rice.

Lemon-butter sauce can be used on most steamed vegetables and is particularly good on zucchini, yellow squash, string beans, cauliflower, and Brussels sprouts, or as a dip for artichokes.

GARDEN FRESH PEAS AND LETTUCE

¼ cup fresh butter
 1 clove garlic
 3 cups freshly shelled peas (about 3 lbs. in the shell), or 1
    16-oz. bag frozen peas
 1 head romaine, red leaf, butter, or iceberg lettuce
¼ tsp. basil
¼ tsp. thyme
¾ cup water
    Sea salt, seasoned salt, or salt-free seasoning to taste

This is a particularly good main course when fresh peas are in season in the spring. Peas are a fairly concentrated vegetable and are therefore quite filling.

Melt the butter in a heavy saucepan. Cut the garlic into two or three pieces. Add it to the butter and sauté it for a few minutes over low heat. Remove the garlic pieces. Add the peas. Continue cooking and stirring to coat them with the butter. Coarsely chop the lettuce and add it to the peas. Add the herbs and water and bring to a boil, stirring constantly. Reduce the heat to medium-low, cover the saucepan, and cook the peas 10 minutes for frozen to 25 minutes for fresh. Uncover and continue cooking a few more minutes until all the water is absorbed. Add seasoned salt and more butter to taste. This amount is enough for a main course for 2 to 3 people.

MIXED STEAMED VEGETABLES I

The following recipe is an example of combinations of vegetables. Following the basic directions, try other combinations that might appeal to you.

1 bunch broccoli
1 head cauliflower
2 large yellow squash
¼ cup raw butter or unrefined safflower, sunflower, or corn oil
2 Tbs. fresh-squeezed lemon juice or 1 Tbs. tamari
1 Tbs. unhulled sesame seeds (optional)

Cut the heavy ends of the stalks from the broccoli, leaving the flower and 2 to 3 inches of the stem. Slice each stalk lengthwise using the individual flowerettes as a guide. The pieces should be ½ to 1 inch thick. Remove the core from the cauliflower and cut the head into large flowerettes. Slice the yellow squash in ½-inch thicknesses. Place the cauliflower in a steamer tray over boiling water. Steam 5 minutes. Add the broccoli and the squash and continue steaming another 7 to 10 minutes, until all the vegetables are just tender.

There are several possible sauces for mixed steamed vegetables. You can use the lemon-butter sauce I have already described, adding 2 Tbs. fresh lemon juice to ¼ cup melted butter. If you wish to avoid the use of butter, you can whip together ¼ cup unrefined oil and 2 Tbs. lemon juice or ¼ cup unrefined oil and 1 Tbs. tamari. Sprinkle with sesame seeds. Serves 6.

MIXED STEAMED VEGETABLES II

    1 lb. fresh string beans
    2 large carrots
    2 Tbs. unrefined safflower oil
  ½ cup water
    1 bunch broccoli
  ¼ cup fresh butter or unrefined oil
    1 Tbs. fresh-squeezed lemon juice
      Seasoned salt or salt-free seasoning to taste

Wash the string beans and trim the ends off. Cut the carrots into quarters and then into ½-inch pieces. Heat the oil in a heavy saucepan. Add the carrots to the oil and stir to coat well. Add the string beans and stir to coat. Add the water, cover the pan tightly, and steam the vegetables for 10 minutes over medium heat. Trim the heavy ends of the stalks from the broccoli, leaving the flower and 2 to 3 inches of the stem. Cut the broccoli into thin pieces, and add it to the other vegetables. Cover and continue steaming another 10 minutes until all the vegetables are tender but retain their bright color. Transfer to a large serving bowl. Add melted butter or oil, lemon juice, and seasoned salt, and mix well. Serves 6.

TORTILLA BOOGIE

This is the ultimate in the steamed vegetable meal, combining an assortment of steamed vegetables with fresh, hot corn tortillas and alfalfa sprouts. It is filling and satisfying and a perfect transition diet meal when salad and steamed vegetables are not enough. Corn tortillas are an excellent substitute for bread, since they contain no yeast and are considerably lighter. They are usually made from corn meal and water and a trace of lime. A fabulous whole wheat tortilla is also available from Garden of Eatin'.

Tortillas are becoming more and more popular nowadays, and you can probably find a tortilleria in your area that makes them fresh daily. Garden of Eatin', the people who make chapatis and whole wheat tortillas, also make excellent tortillas from yellow corn and blue corn, which are more nutritious than the white corn variety. See p. 31 for more information on flatbreads.

We call this meal the Tortilla Boogie because unless you have an electric frying pan or a crepe maker that you can plug in right at your dinner table, you must go back and forth to the kitchen to heat your tortillas. The tortillas should be consumed hot off the frying pan, each one heated individually as you eat it. We have found this meal to be the most fun when eaten in the kitchen.

Choose three or four of the following vegetables:

    2 lbs. asparagus
    2 bunches of broccoli
    4 yellow squash
    1 large cauliflower
    1 lb. Brussels sprouts
    1 lb. fresh mushrooms

• • •

    1 head iceberg, romaine, or red leaf lettuce
    3 cups fresh alfalfa sprouts
      Butter, mustard, mayonnaise
      Seasoned salt or salt-free seasoning to taste
2 to 3 packages corn tortillas (allow 3 to 4 tortillas per person)

Prepare the vegetables. Break off the heavy asparagus stalks. Trim the heavy ends of the stalks from the broccoli, leaving the flower and 2 to 3 inches of the stem. Cut the broccoli into long, thin flowerettes; cut the yellow squash into ½-inch chunks. Remove the core from the cauliflower and cut the head into chunks. Trim the ends off the Brussels sprouts. If you choose to use mushrooms, prepare them as for Basic Sautéed Mushrooms.

Place the vegetables (except the mushrooms) in the top of a vegetable steamer over boiling water. If you are using cauliflower or Brussels sprouts, steam them 5 to 10 minutes before adding the broccoli or squash. Steam all the vegetables until they are tender when pierced with a sharp knife. Cut the cauliflower into bite-sized pieces and slice the Brussels sprouts in half. Place all of the vegetables in a large bowl.

Separate the lettuce leaves, wash and dry them thoroughly, and arrange them in a large wooden bowl. Place a generous amount of fresh alfalfa sprouts in the center.

Heat a small or medium-sized frying pan over high heat until it is *very* hot and then lower the heat.

Now you are ready to assemble the tortillas, and this should be done by each individual according to his or her own taste. Heat a corn tortilla on the preheated frying pan until it is pliable, *but not crisp.*

If you are using condiments, spread a small amount of soft butter, mustard, or mayonnaise on the hot tortilla. Add a leaf of lettuce and then arrange a selection of the steamed vegetables down the center. Top with alfalfa sprouts and seasoned salt. Now roll the tortilla tightly around the filling so that it can be held comfortably in one hand.

When eating Tortilla Boogie, do not hesitate to return to the frying pan several times. You will probably want to try several different combinations of vegetables and condiments to see which is your favorite. Eat as many tortillas as you like, until you are pleasantly full, and even then you may want to have "the old one more." Enjoy yourself! This is basically a vegetable meal. It is extremely cleansing (as long as you do not overeat), and, if you enjoy it, it can become one of the most important meals in your transition diet. Serves 4 to 6.

VEGETABLE STEW

  1 Tbs. unrefined safflower oil
  1 Tbs. fresh butter
  1 clove garlic
  1 onion
  1 large carrot
½ lb. fresh string beans
  2 cups fresh peas
  1 cauliflower
  1 vegetable bouillon cube
  1 tsp. cornstarch
1½ cups water
¼ tsp. thyme
½ tsp. seasoned salt or salt-free seasoning

Heat the oil and the butter in a heavy saucepan. Mince the garlic and chop the onion. Add them to the saucepan and sauté briefly. Cut the carrot into small cubes; cut the string beans in 1-inch pieces. Add the carrot, the string beans, and the peas to the saucepan and sauté, stirring frequently. Cut the core out of the cauliflower and break the head into small flowerettes. Add these to the saucepan and mix well. Add the vegetable bouillon. Dissolve the cornstarch in the water and add this to the saucepan. Mix well to dissolve the bouillon. Add the thyme and the seasoned salt. Bring the sauce to a boil, lower the heat, and simmer the vegetable stew, covered, 20 minutes or until all the vegetables are tender. If the sauce becomes too thick during cooking, add ½ to 1 cup more water. Serve the vegetable stew over Steamed Butternut Squash or over mashed potatoes. It can also be accompanied by Crusty Potatoes. Serves 3 to 4.

STEAMED BUTTERNUT SQUASH

1 butternut squash
  Fresh butter to taste

Cut the squash into large chunks, remove the seeds, and place the chunks in the top of a vegetable steamer over boiling water. Cover and steam 20 minutes to ½ hour or until the squash is tender. Remove the cover, allow the squash to cool slightly, and then scrape it from the shell. Mash it and add fresh butter to taste. Serves 3 to 4.

STEAMED ARTICHOKES

Artichokes are delicious and easy to make. Although they themselves are not heavy, they are extremely filling when you are craving something heavy. Make them the main part of your meal and cook two per person, if desired. When selecting artichokes, choose the ones whose petals have not opened far. The tighter, more compact the artichoke, the fresher it will be.

4 large fresh artichokes
¼ cup fresh butter
1 Tbs. fresh-squeezed lemon juice (optional)

Trim the ends of the heavy artichoke stem and snip the thorny tip off each petal. Wash them and shake out the excess water. Place them in a vegetable steamer over boiling water. Keep the water at a low boil so that it does not boil away.

Steam the artichokes 35 to 45 minutes, depending on their size. They are ready when one of the outer petals can be removed easily. Drain them and cool them slightly before serving.

Melt the butter and add the lemon juice, if desired. Four large artichokes will serve 2, 3, or 4 people, depending on what else you are serving and how hungry you are.

For those who have never eaten an artichoke, it is a simple procedure. The petals are removed one by one from the stalk, outer petals first. Each petal as it is removed is dipped in butter, and the lower portion of the petal, the part which is tender, is eaten by pulling the petal between the teeth. When you have eaten all the petals, you will notice a furlike substance remaining on the top of the stalk. This is the center of the flower (choke). Remove it with a knife (never eat it because it sticks in the throat!), and you are left with the artichoke heart. This can be cut into sections, dipped, and eaten. This is the most filling part of the artichoke.

Variation: Artichokes can be dipped in mayonnaise as well as butter. Homemade mayonnaise makes a particularly good dip.

FRENCH STYLE
JULIENNED STRING BEANS

1 lb. fresh string beans
2 Tbs. fresh butter or an equal amount of unrefined olive or safflower oil
1 clove garlic
1 cup water
Sea salt, seasoned salt, or salt-free seasoning to taste
Squeeze of fresh lemon juice (optional)

Cut the string beans into long thin strips, removing the ends. (Most kitchen specialty shops sell a small gadget for julienning string beans that costs about 75¢.) Melt the butter or heat the oil in a heavy saucepan. Cut the garlic clove into slices and add it to the oil. Add the string beans and stir to coat with oil. Add the water, bringing it to a boil, and cover. Simmer 15 minutes over low heat or until the string beans are tender. Add sea salt or seasoned salt and a squeeze of fresh lemon juice. This amount is enough for a main course for 2 to 3 people, or the string beans are delicious cooled and tossed into the Basic Everyday Salad.

GARLIC STRING BEANS

Whenever I am cooking this dish, I am reminded of the old-fashioned pot roast I used to make. I think it must be the process of slightly searing the beans in oil with garlic that conjures up old memories, but that is where the comparison ends. For when you sit down to a big bowl of buttery garlic string beans—as your main course!—you immediately appreciate how much lighter and more satisfying it is than a heavy, long-cooked piece of beef. This simple dish is one of my family's favorites.

   2 lbs. fresh string beans
   3 Tbs. unrefined safflower oil
   2 cloves garlic
½ tsp. thyme
     Seasoned salt or salt-free seasoning to taste
   1 vegetable bouillon cube
1½ cups water
   2 Tbs. fresh butter (optional)

Trim or break the ends off the beans and snap or cut them into 1-inch pieces. Heat the oil in a large, heavy saucepan. Mince the garlic and add it to the oil. Sauté the garlic briefly but do not let it brown. Add the green beans and stir well over high heat until all of the beans are well coated with oil and are beginning to sear. Add the thyme, the seasoned salt, and the vegetable bouillon. Mix well. Add the water and bring to a boil, stirring until the bouillon dissolves. Cover tightly and reduce the heat to medium-low. Simmer the string beans for approximately 20 minutes or until they are quite tender. A rich sauce will have formed. This amount will fill 4 large bowls. Half a tablespoon of fresh butter can be added to each serving.

MOM'S CAULIFLOWER

The advantage to this simple, tasty cauliflower dish is that the cauliflower can be prepared in advance and reheated in a casserole dish in the oven before serving.

1 large head cauliflower
1 cup of water
1 Tbs. fresh-squeezed lemon juice
2 Tbs. fresh butter
¼ cup whole wheat bread crumbs
Pinch of bouquet garni
Sea salt to taste

Remove the heavy core from the cauliflower and cut the head into flowerettes. Place the flowerettes in a medium-sized saucepan with the water and lemon juice. Bring the water to a boil, cover, and simmer the cauliflower 15 minutes or until tender when pierced with a sharp knife. Do not overcook the cauliflower and allow it to become mushy! At this point you can drain the vegetable and set it aside until you are ready to do your final meal preparation.

Preheat the oven to 350 degrees. Arrange the cauliflower in an ovenproof casserole. Melt the butter and pour it over the cauliflower. Sprinkle the bread crumbs and bouquet garni on top. Add sea salt to taste. Place the casserole in the oven for 15 minutes or until the cauliflower is heated through. This makes a good accompaniment to a large salad and serves 2. Do not use cheese in the salad because of the presence of the bread crumbs.

STEAMED ZUCCHINI

2 lbs. fresh zucchini, preferably the smaller, more flavorful variety
2 Tbs. unrefined olive oil
½ tsp. dried basil
½ cup water
Fresh butter and seasoned salt or salt-free seasoning to taste

Cut the zucchini into ¼-inch slices, discarding the ends. Heat the oil in a large, heavy saucepan, add the zucchini slices, and stir to coat with oil. Add the dried basil and the water, bringing the water to a boil. Cover and simmer the zucchini over medium-low heat for approximately 5 minutes or until it is just tender. When it begins to lose its chalky yellow color and becomes translucent, it is ready. With a slotted spoon transfer the vegetable to 2 or 3 individual wooden bowls. Add fresh butter and seasoned salt to taste.

Zucchini is so full of water that you can eat quite a large quantity and not feel that you have overeaten. When you have eaten nothing but fruit all day, a large bowl of buttered zucchini (or, if you are eliminating butter, add some olive oil) and a Basic Everyday Salad with olives is an extremely satisfying and *cleansing* meal.

Variation: Yellow squash and summer squash can be prepared exactly as you prepare zucchini.

BAKED ACORN SQUASH

2 acorn squash
2 Tbs. fresh butter
4 tsp. raw honey
  Nutmeg to taste

Preheat the oven to 375 degrees.

Cut the squash in half and remove the seeds. Arrange the halves in a shallow baking dish. In each half place ½ Tbs. butter, 1 tsp. honey, and a dash of nutmeg. Pour ½ cup water into the baking dish, cover the dish tightly with aluminum foil, and bake the squash for 1 hour or until they are tender when pierced with a sharp knife. Fluff the squash in the shells with a fork. Serves 2 as a main course or 4 as an accompaniment to Garlic String Beans and a salad.

PEA AND MUSHROOM CASSEROLE

¼ cup fresh butter
1 small onion, thinly sliced
½ lb. fresh mushrooms, sliced
1 head romaine or iceberg lettuce, cut into small chunks
3 cups freshly shelled peas
1 tsp. basil
  Seasoned salt or salt-free seasoning to taste

Melt the butter in a heavy ovenproof casserole. Add the onion and sauté until transparent. Add the mushrooms and sauté briefly to coat with the melted butter. Add the lettuce and mix well. Add the peas, the basil, and the water. Bring to a boil, reduce the heat to medium, and cover tightly. Simmer 15 to 20 minutes until the peas are tender and the lettuce is fully wilted. Add a dash of seasoned salt to taste. Serve Pea and Mushroom Casserole as a topping for steamed brown rice, couscous, or basmati rice. You will love it. This amount serves 3 to 4.

BEST CREAMED CORN EVER

6 ears fresh corn, or 1 16-oz. bag frozen corn kernels
2 Tbs. fresh butter
2 Tbs. whole wheat pastry flour
½ cup water from steamed corn
½ tsp. turmeric
½ cup all-purpose or raw cream
½ tsp. seasoned salt or salt-free seasoning

Steam the ears of corn in a vegetable steamer over boiling water for 5 minutes. Allow them to cool briefly and cut off the kernels. If using frozen corn, prepare the sauce, adding the frozen kernels at the end. Melt the butter in a heavy saucepan. Add the flour and stir to blend. Add the water and stir until a smooth paste forms. Add the turmeric, the raw cream, and the seasoned salt, and continue stirring to form a thick sauce. Stir in the corn and simmer for several minutes to combine the flavors. Do not boil. Serves 2 to 3.

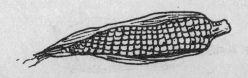

GREG'S FAVORITE (WINTER) SUCCOTASH

- 2 cups dried lima beans
- 7 cups water
- 3 cups diced carrots
- 3 cups freshly shelled peas (or frozen, if fresh are not available), or 3 cups fresh string beans cut into 1-inch pieces
- 3 cups fresh corn (cut from cob) or 1 16-oz. bag frozen corn
- 1 vegetable bouillon cake
- ¼ cup fresh butter
- ½ tsp. sea salt, seasoned salt, or salt-free seasoning

Thoroughly wash the limas and place them in a large, heavy saucepan with the water. Bring to a boil and allow to boil for 1 minute. Turn off the heat and soak the beans, covered, in the water, for several hours if you have the time or for at least 1 hour minimum. When the limas are partially tender, you can begin to prepare the other vegetables.

In the same water in which they have been soaking, bring the lima beans to a boil. Reduce the heat and simmer them, covered, over medium-low heat until they are tender, approximately 30 minutes to an hour, depending on how long they have been soaking. Add the carrots and the peas or string beans and simmer 15 minutes. Add the corn and simmer another 5 to 10 minutes. Add the vegetable bouillon and stir until it has dissolved. Add the butter and the salt and stir until all the ingredients are well blended. This amount serves 4 or 5 as a main course and combines well with the Basic Everyday Salad.

BASIC SAUTEED MUSHROOMS

   1 lb. fresh mushrooms (for maximum freshness, select
      mushrooms whose caps have not opened from the
      stems)
   2 Tbs. unrefined safflower or olive oil, or 1 Tbs. oil and 1
      Tbs. butter
   ½ tsp. seasoned salt or salt-free seasoning (optional)
      Pinch of thyme or basil
1 to 2 Tbs. fresh-squeezed lemon juice (to taste)

Wash the mushrooms gently. Be careful not to overwash
them or they will become soggy. Heat the oil in a large
skillet. Trim the ends off the mushroom stems and thin-
slice the mushrooms into the skillet. Sauté over medium
heat until all the mushrooms have been coated with oil
and they are just beginning to change color. They should
be only slightly soft. Remove the skillet from the heat and
stir in the seasoned salt, thyme, and lemon juice.

Sautéed mushrooms can be used as a sauce for any
steamed vegetable, and they are a real treat in Tortilla
Boogie. They can also be combined with steamed grains
such as brown rice, couscous, kasha, or basmati rice.
Serves 3 to 4.

STUFFED MUSHROOMS

This dish can be treated as a main course and accompanied with a steamed vegetable dish, a steamed grain, and/or a large salad. It combines well with Caesar Salad or Garden Fresh Peas and Lettuce.

12 large or 20 smaller mushrooms with stems
 1 small onion
 1 rib celery
 2 Tbs. unrefined olive oil
 2 cloves garlic
½ tsp. dried sage
¼ tsp. thyme
    Seasoned salt or salt-free seasoning to taste
 2 Tbs. chopped fresh parsley
 2 Tbs. fresh-squeezed lemon juice
¼ cup fresh butter

Remove the stems from the mushrooms. Gently wash the caps and set them aside to drain on a paper towel. Chop together until very fine the stems, the onion, and the celery.

Heat the olive oil in a large, heavy skillet. Add the chopped vegetables and sauté lightly. Use a garlic press to crush 1 clove of the garlic and add it to the chopped vegetables. Mix well. Add the sage, thyme, and seasoned salt. Continue sautéing over medium heat for several minutes until the stuffing mixture softens. Stir in the parsley and lemon juice. Remove from the heat and set aside.

Preheat the oven to 400 degrees. Melt the butter and add the second clove of garlic, crushed. Fill each mushroom cap with a generous spoonful of stuffing and place it in a shallow casserole dish. Pour the garlic butter over the mushrooms. Bake 20 minutes until the mushrooms are tender and the aroma fills the kitchen. Place under the broiler for a few minutes to brown. This amount serves 3.

POTATOES

Potatoes can be quite important during the winter months, especially if you are living in a cold climate. There will be chilly nights when you will crave something heavy, and the potato will be it. Potatoes, however, are not in themselves inordinately heavy. They have earned that false reputation as a result of improper food combining. Since they are traditionally combined with meat, chicken, or fish, they are blamed for the heavy feeling that results from the overburdened digestive system working on incompatible protein and carbohydrate foods simultaneously. The rule to remember is that *potatoes should never be combined with any protein food.* They must be treated as the main dish of any meal and accompanied by vegetables or salad, high-water-content foods that will aid in their speedy digestion. Eaten in this way, you will find the delicious potato—be it baked, boiled, roasted, or pan-fried—in all of its varieties, to be one of your best cool weather friends.

BAKED IDAHOS, SWEET POTATOES, OR YAMS

> 4 large potatoes
> ¼ cup butter
> Sour cream (optional, and not recommended)

Preheat the oven to 400 degrees. Wash and thoroughly dry the potatoes and place them in a shallow baking pan. Bake 1 to 1½ hours or until the potatoes are thoroughly soft. If you are inserting large potato skewers to conduct the heat, (these are available in most household departments and at some hardware stores), the baking time will be cut approximately in half. Cool the potatoes 15 minutes. Slice open along the top and mash 1 Tbs. fresh butter into each potato. Serves 4. Remember to expedite the digestion of these buttery potatoes by eating them with a large salad.

PARSLEYED NEW POTATOES

> 2 lbs. new potatoes (new potatoes are those with the red skins)
> ¼ cup fresh butter
> 2 Tbs. finely chopped fresh parsley
> Seasoned salt or salt-free seasoning to taste

Steam or boil the potatoes in their skins until they are just tender when pierced with a sharp knife. (It is possible to steam new potatoes on a vegetable steamer tray in the same way that you steam other vegetables. They tend to have more flavor than when they are boiled. If they are small, it does not take more than about 20 minutes.) Cool the potatoes slightly and then remove the skins. Melt the butter in a heavy skillet. Add the potatoes and shake the skillet to coat them with butter. Add the chopped parsley and the seasoned salt and continue shaking the pan until the potatoes are well coated. The parsley should retain its fresh green color. This amount serves 3 to 4 and combines well with a large salad (without cheese!) and a green steamed vegetable with lemon-butter sauce.

Note: This is not recommended for nursing mothers since parsley has the effect of drying up the milk.

CRUSTY POTATOES

  2 lbs. new potatoes
 ¼ cup fresh butter
     Dash of paprika
 ½ tsp. seasoned salt or salt-free seasoning

Steam or boil the potatoes until they are just tender but not quite done. Cool in the skins and then remove the skins. Melt the butter in a medium-sized casserole in a 400-degree oven. Add the potatoes. Sprinkle with the paprika and seasoned salt. Bake, turning in the butter, for 45 minutes or until a crispy crust has formed. These crusty potatoes are extremely tasty and combine well with any mixed steamed vegetable dish and a salad (without cheese!) for a hearty winter's meal. Serves 3 or 4.

HASH BROWNS

                2 lbs. all-purpose new or White Rose potatoes
                2 Tbs. unrefined olive or safflower oil
½ to 1 tsp. seasoned salt or salt-free seasoning

Wash and dry the potatoes. It is not necessary to peel
them. Heat the oil in a large, heavy skillet. Coarsely chop
the potatoes and add them to the oil. Sauté them, stirring
frequently, cutting them with the sharp end of the spatula
until a crust begins to form. Press the potatoes down into
the skillet, sprinkle them with seasoned salt, and allow
them to fry until they are crusty on one side. Turn them
carefully with the spatula, press them down again, and
sprinkle with with more seasoned salt. Allow them to
brown and crisp to the desired doneness. Serve with a
large salad or mix them directly into the salad. Serves 3
or 4.

SUMMER SUCCOTASH

1½ lbs. new potatoes
3 large ears fresh corn
¼ cup fresh butter
4 carrots
2 cups freshly shelled peas
1 cup boiling water
1 vegetable bouillon cube
1 bunch broccoli
½ tsp. seasoned salt or salt-free seasoning
½ tsp. thyme

Steam or boil the potatoes in their skins until tender. Cool them, remove the skins, and cut them into cubes. Set the potatoes aside while you prepare the other vegetables. Cut the kernels from the corn and set them aside. Melt the butter in a large, heavy saucepan. Cut the carrots into small cubes and add them to the butter. Add the fresh peas and boiling water, in which you have dissolved the vegetable bouillon. Bring to a boil and simmer, covered, 10 minutes. Cut the broccoli into small flowerettes, reserving the stalks for Cream of Broccoli Soup. Add the broccoli, the cubed potatoes, and the fresh corn to the other vegetables. Season with seasoned salt and thyme. Bring to a boil and simmer, covered, over medium-low heat until all of the vegetables are tender. This should take approximately 10 minutes. Serve in large wooden bowls and pass more butter to taste. A large Basic Everyday Salad combines well with Summer Succotash. Serves 4.

GRAINS

As you move from lighter foods such as salads and vegetable dishes to heavier meals, the unrefined whole grains will become an integral part of your transition diet. There are many to choose from: brown rice, millet, basmati rice, couscous, barley, buckwheat groats or kasha, triticale or wheat berries, to name just a few. In our own diet, I have found brown rice, basmati rice, barley, couscous, and kasha to be an adequate selection.

Brown rice is a completely whole food, rich in many of the nutritional elements necessary for good health. Unlike white rice it is hulled in such a way as to protect the important outer bran layers. There are three types. Long grain brown rice is light and fluffy. The medium grain is moist, and the short grain has a nutty flavor and tends to clump together. Each has a distinctive quality, and you should try them all to appreciate the variety. This important point about brown rice is made on page 323 in *The Deaf Smith Country Cookbook:* "Rice is one crop that is more expensive to grow organically. You can be sure that cheap brown rice is not organically grown. Most commercial rice farming entails ecologically unsound practices and staggering amounts of poisons. Commercial rice is one of the most heavily chemicalized food crops. Be especially careful of your source of brown rice. The name of every organic rice supplier is well known, so ask."

From start to finish, brown rice requires about 1 hour of preparation time. It is a satisfying accompaniment to steamed vegetables or salad and a perfect food for growing children.

Basmati rice I find to be relatively new on the natural food scene. It is an unrefined white rice from Pakistan. It is lighter than brown rice and has a distinctive flavor and aroma that is hard to resist. It requires approximately 20 minutes of preparation time and is delicious in salads or combined with steamed vegetables.

Barley should be purchased in natural foods stores, for commercial barleys have been pearled to the point where most of the important nutritional elements have been removed with the outer layers. Barley should be brown, not white. It is quite a heavy grain, and I find that it is most easily digested in soups. Barley requires about 1 hour and 10 minutes of preparation time.

Couscous is a semolina grain from North Africa. Of all the grains, it reminds me most of pasta. There is a simple cooking method for couscous that requires less than 5 minutes from start to finish.

Buckwheat groats or kasha can be purchased preroasted for easier preparation. The whole kasha is the most nutritious. It cooks rapidly in slightly less than half an hour and has a strong flavor that is particularly satisfying in winter. The only drawback that I find to kasha, and it is a big drawback, is that it requires an egg in cooking, which is essentially a poor food combination, and I have yet to develop or find a successful recipe for kasha without the egg. The presence of this protein-carbohydrate combination makes kasha heavier to digest than other grains, so when I use it I prepare a small amount of kasha, which I offset with a large amount of fresh vegetable sauce.

Do not limit your experimentation with grains. Try all those available, as long as they are whole and unprocessed. When it is necessary to add these heavier elements to your diet, the experience can be an adventure in new tastes and textures.

PERFECT BROWN RICE

    1 cup brown rice (long, medium, or short grain)
2¼ cups water
    1 tsp. sea salt
    1 Tbs. unrefined safflower oil

Place all the ingredients in a saucepan with a tight-fitting lid, in the order given. Bring to a boil and stir gently with a fork. Cover and simmer over low heat for 40 minutes. *Do not* lift the lid while the rice is cooking. Remove from the heat and allow to stand 10 to 20 minutes *with the lid on* before serving. Serves 2.

I frequently make 2 or 3 cups of rice, thus tripling the recipe, so that I can have some left over. The leftover can be mixed into salads (do not add cheese!) or it can be used in Wok Fried Rice.

BROWN RICE WITH MUSHROOMS

Prepare brown rice as in the recipe for Perfect Brown Rice. Prepare Basic Sautéed Mushrooms. When the rice is ready, stir in the mushrooms and gravy. Combine with a large salad. Serves 2 to 4.

WOK FRIED RICE

2 Tbs. unrefined safflower, sesame, or peanut oil
1 lb. fresh mushrooms, or 2 cups dried Black Forest
  mushrooms (available in the Oriental food section
  of your supermarket or in some natural foods stores)
1 carrot
1 bunch steamed broccoli, heavy stems removed
6 cups leftover brown rice
1 vegetable bouillon cube, dissolved in 1 cup boiling water, or
  1 cup mushroom liquid
2 Tbs. tamari, or 4 Tbs. soy sauce

If you do not have a wok, you could probably make this dish in a large skillet, but the wok does make the preparation easier.

Heat the oil in a large wok. Slice the mushrooms and add them to the hot oil. (If you are using dried mushrooms, they must be soaked in 2 cups water for at least ½ hour before you begin the rest of your meal preparation. When they are soft, remove the heavy stems and slice the caps. Reserve 1 cup of the soaking liquid for the rice. Strain through a fine sieve or cheesecloth.) Stir fry the mushrooms until they are seared.

Grate the carrot on a coarse grater and add it to the wok. Stir fry until the carrot begins to soften. Cut the steamed broccoli in thin slices (from flowerette to stalk) and add it to the wok. Add the rice and continue stir frying until all the ingredients are well combined. Add the vegetable bouillon dissolved in boiling water or the reserved mushroom water, as much as is necessary to thoroughly moisten the rice. Add the tamari or soy sauce and mix well. This is an ample amount for 4.

WOK FRIED RICE ANOTHER WAY

> 1 clove garlic
> 1 cup fresh or frozen peas
> 1 carrot
> 1 bunch broccoli
> 2 Tbs. unrefined safflower or sesame oil
> ½ cup water
> 1 to 2 Tbs. tamari
> ¼ tsp. Chinese five spice seasoning
> 1 bunch scallions
> ½ lb. fresh mushrooms or ¼ lb. fresh shiitake mushrooms
> 6 cups steamed brown rice
> 2 cups bean sprouts

Prepare the vegetables. Mince the garlic, shell the peas, cut the carrot into pea-sized cubes. Use only the top 2 inches of the broccoli, cutting the flowerettes in thin lengthwise slices. Heat 1 Tbs. of the oil in the wok. Add the garlic and stir fry until it is tender. Add the peas and the carrot and stir fry several minutes. Add the broccoli and continue stir frying until all the vegetables are well coated with oil and bright in color. Add the water and the tamari, stir in the Chinese five spice seasoning, and bring to a boil. Lower the heat, cover, and steam 10 to 15 minutes, stirring periodically.

Meanwhile, prepare the remaining vegetables. Slice the scallions into ½-inch pieces, using some of the green ends. Slice the mushrooms. If you are able to find fresh shiitake mushrooms (usually available at Oriental markets), cut them into large slices, since they tend to break up a little in cooking.

Remove the steamed vegetables and their liquid from the wok. Add the remaining 1 Tbs. of oil to the wok, toss in the scallions, and stir fry until they soften. Add the mushrooms and stir fry briefly. Add the rice, 4 or 5 Tbs. at a time, and continue stir frying until all the rice has been heated thoroughly. Gently mix in the steamed vegetables, reserving the liquid. Mix in the bean sprouts and pour the vegetable liquid over the top. Adjust the seasonings. Cover and steam over low heat for 5 minutes, taking care that the rice does not stick. Serves 3.

BASMATI RICE
WITH FRESH ZUCCHINI SAUCE

The aroma of basmati rice while it is steaming is hard to resist. You will love its special rich flavor. This delicate zucchini sauce is a perfect complement because it allows the flavor of the basmati to come through.

Prepare the basmati:

    2 cups basmati
    4 cups water
1 to 2 Tbs. unrefined safflower oil
    1 tsp. sea salt

Measure the basmati into a large saucepan with a tight-fitting lid. Add the water, oil, and salt. Bring to a boil and stir briefly. Cover tightly and simmer 17 minutes over *low* heat. Remove the lid. Fluff the rice with a fork. This amount serves 3 to 4. Any that is left over can be reserved for use in a salad.

Prepare the zucchini sauce:

3 Tbs. unrefined olive or safflower oil
3 lbs. fresh zucchini, the smaller variety if it is available
1 tsp. oregano
1 vegetable bouillon cube
1 cup water

Heat the oil in a heavy saucepan. Coarsely chop the zucchini and add it to the oil. Sauté it momentarily, stirring well to coat with oil. Add the oregano, vegetable bouillon, and water. Bring to a boil, stirring constantly to dissolve the bouillon. Reduce the heat and simmer, tightly covered, for approximately 5 to 10 minutes, or until the zucchini is tender and forms a rich sauce. Spoon over bowls of hot basmati. Serves 4.

A HEARTY WINTER MEAL

    2 Tbs. unrefined safflower oil
    2 carrots, cut into chunks
    2 stalks celery, sliced
    1 clove garlic, minced
   12 dried mushrooms, presoaked for at least ½ hour
    ½ tsp. curry (optional)
    1 cup brown rice
    ½ cup lentils
    ½ cup split peas
    2 zucchini, sliced
    6 cups water
    2 cups mushroom broth, strained through cheesecloth
    1 vegetable bouillon cube

In a large, heavy saucepan, heat the oil and add the carrots, celery, and garlic. Slice the mushrooms, discarding the heavy stems, and add them to the oil. Add the curry. Add the rice, lentils, and split peas and stir well to coat with oil. Add the zucchini, water, mushroom broth, and vegetable bouillon, and bring the mixture to a boil. Stir well to dissolve the bouillon, cover tightly, and simmer over low heat for 50 minutes. This is a wonderful, filling, and nutritious meal that children love. Serves 4 and combines well with a mixed green salad.

VEGETABLE COUSCOUS

- 1 onion, sliced
- ½ cup finely chopped celery
- 2 large carrots, sliced into ⅛-inch rounds
- 2 cups freshly shelled peas (or frozen, if fresh are not available)
- 1 large cauliflower, cut into small flowerettes
- 1 vegetable bouillon cube
- 2 cups boiling water
- 1 large bunch broccoli, cut into small flowerettes
- 1 large or 3 small zucchini, sliced
- 6 small new potatoes, parboiled and sliced (optional)
- 2 Tbs. fresh butter
- 2 Tbs. unrefined safflower oil
- ½ tsp. thyme
- 1 box or 2 cups couscous (found in natural foods stores or the gourmet section of your grocery store)
- 2 cups boiling water
- ¼ cup fresh butter
- 1 tsp. sea salt, seasoned salt, or salt-free seasoning

Prepare all the vegetables. In a large, heavy saucepan, melt the butter and heat the oil. Add the onion and the celery and sauté over low heat until soft. Add the sliced carrots and cook for several minutes, stirring frequently. Add the peas and the cauliflower. Dissolve the vegetable bouillon in boiling water and pour it over the vegetables. Cover and simmer 5 minutes over low heat. Add the broccoli and continue simmering, covered, over low heat for another 5 minutes. Add the zucchini and the sliced parboiled potatoes and continue simmering, covered, another 5 minutes or until all the vegetables are tender but not mushy.

Prepare the couscous:
  I have found that most packages of couscous have a set

of simple directions you can follow. The following procedure works well for me. Place the entire contents of the
package in a heavy saucepan. Add 2 cups boiling water, ¼
cup butter, and 1 tsp. sea salt or seasoned salt. Bring to a
boil, stirring constantly, until all of the water is absorbed
and the couscous is fluffy.

To serve, combine the couscous with the vegetables and
mix well. Spoon into large wooden bowls. This amount
serves 4 to 6 and is delicious left over.

This particular recipe is like a vegetable stew, but any
steamed vegetable can be served as a sauce for couscous.
You can use either of the sauces recommended for kasha,
zucchini sauce, or plain mixed steamed vegetables. Or
have the couscous by itself as a side dish accompaniment
to Steamed Broccoli With Lemon-Butter Sauce and salad.
The combinations and possibilities are infinite.

STEAMED KASHA

2 cups kasha
2 eggs, lightly beaten
4 cups boiling water
2 Tbs. unrefined safflower oil
1 tsp. sea salt

Mix the kasha and the eggs together in a bowl. Add the
mixture to a dry, hot wok or a large, heavy skillet with a
tight-fitting lid. Stir until the egg dissipates. Add the boiling
water, the oil, and the salt. Stir briefly. Reduce the heat to
low, cover, and steam ½ hour. This amount serves 4 to 5.

If you do have a wok, be sure to use it when you prepare
kasha. It comes out lighter and fluffier.

MIXED VEGETABLE SAUCE FOR KASHA

    2 Tbs. unrefined safflower oil
    2 cloves garlic
    1 onion
    1 stalk celery
    2 large carrots
    1 lb. string beans
    1 cauliflower
    1 vegetable bouillon cube
    1 cup water
  ½ tsp. bouquet garni
    Seasoned salt or salt-free seasoning to taste

Heat the oil in a heavy saucepan. Mince the garlic and chop the onion and add them to the hot oil. Lower the heat and sauté until soft. Chop the celery and the carrots and add them to the oil. Remove the ends from the string beans and cut them in ¼- to ½-inch pieces. Remove the heavy core from the cauliflower and chop the head. Add the string beans and the cauliflower to the saucepan and stir well to coat all the vegetables with oil. Add the bouillon and the water, bring to a boil, and stir until the bouillon is dissolved. Add the bouquet garni and the seasoned salt and simmer, covered, over low heat, for 15 minutes or until all the vegetables are tender.

To serve, combine the kasha and the vegetable sauce in a large serving bowl or in your wok and allow people to help themselves. This amount of sauce is enough for 4 people.

This sauce can also be used on brown rice, basmati, or couscous.

BROCCOLI-POTATO SAUCE FOR KASHA

         2 Tbs. unrefined safflower oil
         2 cloves garlic
         1 onion
         2 carrots
         1 stalk celery
3 or 4 large new potatoes
         1 vegetable bouillon cube
     1½ cups water
         4 cups coarsely chopped broccoli (1 large or 2 small
            bunches), heavy stems removed
         1 tsp. bouquet garni
            Seasoned salt or salt-free seasoning to taste

The combination of the small amount of potatoes in this sauce and the kasha is a surprising taste treat.

Heat the oil in a large, heavy saucepan. Mince the garlic, chop the onion, and add them to the oil. Chop the carrots and the celery and cube the potatoes, and after the garlic and onion have sautéed for a few minutes, add these other vegetables. Sauté several minutes until all the vegetables begin to soften. Add the vegetable bouillon and the water, bring the mixture to a boil, lower the heat, and simmer, covered, for 10 minutes. Add the broccoli, the bouquet garni, and the seasoned salt, and simmer, covered, for another 10 minutes. The vegetables should all be tender and the sauce should be quite thick. To serve, mix the sauce in with the steamed kasha or spoon it over individual bowls of kasha. Serves 4. Because of the heavy carbohydrates in this dish, it is best to combine it with a large salad.

6

WEEKEND AND HOLIDAY FEASTS

Joyous Meals That Are Fun to Prepare

Feasting is an integral part of our social tradition. Unfortunately, in recent years, people have lost interest in the homemade feast and have turned more and more toward the practice of going to restaurants. Restaurant dining has its place, but the care and joy you put into meal preparation for yourself and your loved ones and friends yield health benefits that cannot come to you from restaurant eating. In these days of microwave ovens and chemically treated food, it is more important than ever that you take control of what goes into your food and how it is prepared.

FEASTING

The recipes that follow are special ideas for weekends, parties, or holiday eating. Most of them require a longer preparation time than do salads, plain vegetables, or grains. And as is usually the case in these matters, most of them require a longer digestion time. Try these recipes when you have enough time to prepare them enjoyably and adequate rest time to allow your body to deal with them. You will find them fun to make and fun to eat.

I have tried in these pages to develop interesting and original alternatives to restaurant menus, so that if you are tempted to dine out, you may opt for preparing some new and exciting dish at home.

CALIFORNIA TOSTADA

This beautiful main-course salad contains *everything* and is a festive Mexican-style meal that makes an ideal lunch for entertaining. If you are serving it as part of a Mexican buffet, you can accompany it with steamed brown rice and refried pinto beans.

- 2 cups string beans, cut into 1-inch pieces, or freshly shelled peas if they are available
- 2 cups carrot rounds
- 2 cups cauliflower flowerettes
- 2 cups broccoli flowerettes
- 1 head iceberg or romaine lettuce
- 1 bunch spinach
- 1 cucumber
- 2 large tomatoes, or approximately 2 cups halved cherry tomatoes
- 2 cups alfalfa sprouts
- ½ tsp. seasoned salt or salt-free seasoning
- ½ tsp. oregano
  Pinch of thyme
- 1 cup sour cream
- ¼ cup honey-sweetened ketchup
- ¾ cup mayonnaise
- 2 packages natural-style corn chips
- 16 green or black olives
- 1 ripe avocado, cut into wedges

Place the green beans or peas and the carrots in a vegetable steamer tray over boiling water and steam for 10 minutes. Add the cauliflower and the broccoli and continue steaming another 10 minutes or until all the vegetables are tender. Set them aside to cool while you prepare the salad.

Break the lettuce into bite-sized pieces. Chop the spinach and combine it with the lettuce in a large wooden bowl. Peel and quarter the cucumber and cut it into ½-inch pieces. Cut the tomatoes into small wedges. Add the cucumber and the tomatoes to the greens. Arrange the alfalfa sprouts around the rim of the bowl (so that they won't wilt when you add the cooked vegetables), and add the seasoned salt, the oregano, and the thyme.

Whip together the simple ketchup and mayonnaise dressing. There are so many other flavors in this tostada that a more complicated dressing is not necessary. Be sure, however, that you use one of the sugarless (honey-sweetened) brands found in natural foods stores. They have a superior flavor.

Now you are ready to assemble the tostadas. Add the steamed vegetables to the salad. Pour the dressing on and toss gently but thoroughly. Place a generous quantity of corn chips on each of 4 or 5 large plates. Cover with a heaping serving of salad. Place a dollop of sour cream on top and garnish with olives and avocado wedges.

If you are entertaining in hot weather, this meal is a good choice. Kids love it. It is simple to serve since all that is required is one dish per person.

Variation: Corn can be substituted for any of the vegetables indicated above.

BEAN BURRITOS

2 cups pinto beans
7 cups water
1 clove garlic
1 bay leaf
1 tsp. sea salt
1 cup sour cream
6 whole wheat tortillas or chapatis

Wash the beans carefully and soak them for several hours in water or place the beans in a heavy saucepan, add the water, and bring to a boil. Boil 1 minute and turn off the heat. Allow the beans to stand for 1 hour in the water. When they are partially hydrated, bring the water to a boil again, this time adding the garlic and the bay leaf. Do not add the salt until later for it will toughen the beans. Simmer, covered, over medium-low heat until all the beans are tender, approximately 1½ hours. *Do not drain.*

In the same saucepan in which they have cooked, mash the beans with the back of a large spoon and continue mashing until they have a lumpy consistency and most of the water is incorporated. You can include the garlic clove, which will add to the flavor, but discard the bay leaf. Add the salt and continue mashing, keeping the saucepan at low heat so that the beans do not dry out. When the beans are all mashed to a lumpy consistency, you are ready to assemble the burritos.

In a separate skillet, gently heat a tortilla until it is just warm and pliable. Spoon into the center some beans and a tablespoon of sour cream. Fold opposite sides of the tortilla over the filling and roll the burrito closed. This recipe yields 6 substantial burritos. Two per person is usually enough. Accompany burritos with the Basic Everyday Salad. It will help in the digestion of this rather heavy meal.

ANGEL HAIR PASTA AND
CAULIFLOWER IN BASIL CREAM SAUCE

- 1 cauliflower, cored and cut in thin flowerettes
- 1 lb. vegetable angel hair pasta (spinach, tomato, carrot, green onion, or a combination of one red and one green pasta)
- 5 Tbs. butter
- 1 tsp. minced garlic
- 1 cup heavy all-purpose or raw cream
- ½ tsp. sea salt (optional)
- 1 cup freshly chopped basil
  Freshly ground pepper to taste

Place the cauliflower in a vegetable steamer over boiling water and steam for 5 to 10 minutes or until it is tender when pierced with the tip of a sharp knife. Set aside.

Bring 3 quarts of water to a boil in a large kettle. Add 1 tsp. sea salt, if desired, and 1 Tbs. olive oil. When the water is boiling, slowly add the angel hair, stirring gently to combine the two colors. Cook the pasta only a minute or 2 for fresh, 5 minutes for dried. Drain and toss with 1 Tbs. of the butter.

Melt the remaining butter in a large skillet. Add the garlic and cream. Simmer several minutes until the sauce is reduced. Add the salt and fresh basil and stir well. Add the cauliflower; simmer 2 or 3 minutes to heat the cauliflower through. Pour the sauce over the pasta and toss gently. Add fresh pepper to taste. Serve immediately. Serves 5.

HONEY CORN BREAD

This is the best corn bread recipe ever. I adapted it from one requiring sugar and substituted whole wheat flour for white. The result is a great success. This corn bread combines well with salads or is a fine addition to feasting buffets.

- 1 cup yellow corn meal
- 1 cup whole wheat flour
- ½ tsp sea salt
- 1 tsp. baking powder
- 1 tsp. baking soda
  Slightly less than ¼ cup raw honey
- 1 egg
- 1⅞ cups buttermilk

Preheat the oven to 375 degrees. Heavily butter an 8x8-inch pan.

In a large bowl, combine the dry ingredients. Stir in the liquid ingredients. Mix lightly. Corn bread batter must be a little lumpy. Pour the batter into the prepared pan. Bake for approximately ½ hour, until golden. Be sure to test the bread by inserting a toothpick to see if it comes out clean.

Variation: Substitute ¾ cup yellow corn meal and ¼ cup bran for the 1 cup yellow corn meal.

VEGETABLE PIES AND PASTRIES

I developed the following recipes to satisfy my family's desire for pies and pastries. If you no longer eat cooked fruit because of its extreme acid reaction in the body, you do not have to completely forgo pies or tarts. Just fill them with vegetables! You can't believe how good these are until you try them. The fillings that I suggest are certainly not the only possibilities. Experiment with any ideas that you may have. If you like to bake, preparing vegetable pastries is a great experience. Kids of all ages adore them.

COUNTRY STYLE VEGETABLE PIE

Prepare the flaky pie crust:

> 2 cups whole wheat pastry flour
> ¾ cup fresh butter, softened
> ¼ tsp. sea salt
4 to 6 Tbs. ice water

Cut half of the butter into the flour. Add the salt and the remaining butter and continue cutting until the mixture is grainy. Add ice water one tablespoon at a time and mix with a fork until the pastry begins to come away from the side of the bowl. Knead briefly and form into a ball. Wrap the pastry tightly in wax paper and refrigerate for at least ½ hour.

In the meantime, you can prepare the vegetable filling:

> 3 cups new potatoes (about 5 or 6 medium-sized potatoes)
> 2 cups carrots
> 4 cups broccoli flowerettes (1 bunch)
> ½ cup fresh butter
> 1 small onion, finely chopped
> ¼ cup finely chopped celery
> 2 cups freshly shelled peas
> 3 cups fresh or frozen corn
> ½ tsp. thyme
> ⅛ tsp. sage
> ½ tsp. seasoned salt or salt-free seasoning
> 4 Tbs. flour
> 1 vegetable bouillon cube
> 2 cups all-purpose or raw cream
> ¼ tsp. nutmeg

Steam the potatoes and carrots whole, until tender, then dice into ½-inch pieces. Steam the broccoli flowerettes approximately 5 minutes, until tender-crisp. Melt ¼ cup butter in a large, heavy saucepan. Add the onion and celery, and sauté until soft. Stir in the potatoes and carrots, and cook for several minutes, stirring frequently. Add the peas and broccoli, and cook over low heat for 10 minutes, stirring frequently. Mix in the corn. Add the thyme, sage, and seasoned salt. Allow the vegetable mixture to cool while you are preparing the cream sauce.

Melt the remaining ¼ cup butter. Stir in the flour. Add the vegetable bouillon. Slowly add the cream, stirring constantly until the mixture becomes quite thick. Add the nutmeg. Combine the sauce with the vegetables, mix well, and allow to cool while you roll out the pie crust.

Preheat the oven to 400 degrees. Remove the pastry ball from the refrigerator and cut it in half. On a floured surface, roll out half of the crust to fit a 9½x2-inch-deep Pyrex pie plate. Fill the crust with the vegetables, roll out the second half, and place it gently on top. Seal and flute the edges and prick the top. For a shiny crust, brush lightly with egg white beaten with 1 Tbs. water. Bake for 5 minutes at 400 degrees. Reduce the heat to 375 degrees and bake another 35 to 40 minutes or until the crust is a golden brown.

Serve hot or cooled to room temperature. The cooler the pie is, the better it holds together when it is cut. Accompany with a tossed green salad with lemon and herb dressing. Serves 4 to 6.

SUCCOTASH TURNOVERS

1 recipe Summer Succotash, or 1 recipe Winter Succotash
1 flaky pastry recipe

Prepare the succotash several hours ahead or even the day before. It should be room temperature when you make the turnovers. Winter succotash in particular keeps very well overnight.

Prepare the crust:

Follow the directions for flaky pastry preparation under Country Style Vegetable Pie. Refrigerate the pastry for at least ½ hour so that it is easier to work. Approximately 1½ hours before you are ready to eat, begin to assemble your turnovers.

Preheat the oven to 400 degrees. Remove the chilled dough from the refrigerator. Cut it in half, in quarters, and then in eighths. Or, if you wish to have very small turnovers for a buffet table, cut the ball in half and cut each half in thirds and then in sixths. The first procedure will yield 8 good-sized turnovers; the second, 12 smaller ones. Roll each piece into a ball and then flatten it on a floured board and roll to a ⅛-inch thickness with a rolling pin. Place the desired amount of succotash in the center of the round, fold it in half, and seal the edges with a fork or with your thumb, if you wish the turnovers to have a scalloped shape. Place the finished turnovers on an ungreased cookie sheet and bake them at 400 degrees for 5 minutes. Lower the heat to 375 degrees and bake the turnovers another 25 to 30 minutes, or until they are a golden brown. Cool 20 minutes to ½ hour before serving.

Note: Succotash turnovers are *delicious* cold. If you have any left over, which is unlikely, do not bother to reheat them.

FRENCH VEGETABLE CRESCENT

I developed this recipe one day when I was planning to make my mother-in-law's strudel. I prepared the dough, substituting whole wheat pastry flour for the white flour required in her recipe, and then I found myself faced with the problem of adapting the filling. The more I thought about the filling, the more the idea of a *vegetable strudel* began to appeal to me. This filling came into existence out of the foods that I just happened to have on hand that day, and it worked fantastically well. I called it French Vegetable Crescent because the final shape reminded me of a French croissant.

A word of caution: Be gentle in rolling the dough around the filling. It is a very soft dough and cracks easily. Pinch together or patch any cracks that may form in the rolling. They tend to disappear in the baking.

Crescent dough:

1½ cups whole wheat pastry flour
½ cup fresh butter, softened
½ cup sour cream

Cut the butter into the flour. Add the sour cream and mix together until all the flour is moistened and it is possible to form the dough into a ball. Knead gently until smooth. Wrap tightly in plastic wrap and allow to chill 1 hour while you prepare the filling.

Vegetable filling:

- ¼ cup fresh butter
- 1 small onion
- 1 carrot
- 8 to 10 small new potatoes
- 1 large bunch broccoli
- 1 vegetable bouillon cube
- ½ cup boiling water
- ½ tsp. thyme
- ½ tsp. seasoned salt or salt-free seasoning

Melt the butter in a heavy saucepan. Cut the onion and carrot into very thin slices and sauté until soft. Thinly slice the new potatoes and add them to the saucepan. Continue to cook, stirring frequently until the potatoes soften. Chop the broccoli flowerettes finely. You will need approximately 4 cups. Add the broccoli to the vegetables, cooking and stirring constantly over low heat. Dissolve the vegetable bouillon in the boiling water, add it to the vegetables, and stir well to moisten all the ingredients. Stir in the thyme and the seasoned salt, cover, and simmer over low heat, stirring frequently, until the vegetables have a thick, smooth consistency. This should take about ½ hour. *Allow the filling to cool to room temperature so it does not melt through the dough when you are rolling it.*

To make the crescent:

Preheat the oven to 400 degrees. On a floured piece of wax paper, roll out the pastry into a large circle, ⅛-inch thick. (You can secure the wax paper to your counter surface with tape to make the rolling easier, and use plenty of flour so the pastry does not stick.) Spread the vegetable filling over the top. Roll the pastry gently into a cylindrical shape and then slide it carefully from the wax paper to an ungreased cookie sheet. Curve it into a crescent shape, pinch the ends closed, and pinch together any little cracks that might have formed during the rolling and transfer operations. At this point, for a shinier crust, you can brush the crescent with egg white beaten with 1 Tbs. water. Bake 5 minutes at 400 degrees, reduce the heat to 375 degrees, and continue baking for 35 minutes or until the pastry is lightly browned. Cool at least ½ hour before serving. Serve with a fresh spinach and mushroom salad with a garlic-herb dressing. Serves 4.

Note: French vegetable crescent can be prepared hours in advance or even the day before you need it. It is delicious served at room temperature or reheated for 20 to 30 minutes in a 350-degree oven.

BUTTERMILK CREPES
WITH MUSHROOM CREAM FILLING

Have all the ingredients at room temperature.
Crepe batter:

    1 cup whole wheat pastry flour
    1 egg
    ¾ cup buttermilk
    ½ cup water
    ¼ tsp. sea salt
    2 Tbs. fresh butter, melted

Place the ingredients in a blender container in the order listed above. Blend 30 seconds, stop, and stir down. Blend until smooth, approximately 30 to 60 seconds. Use the batter immediately, or allow it to stand an hour or two for more tender crepes. This amount yields approximately 16 crepes.

Mushroom cream filling:

>   One recipe Basic Sautéed Mushrooms (see Vegetable
>   Dishes and Grains)
>   2 Tbs. fresh butter
>   2 Tbs. whole wheat pastry flour
>   ½ cup water
>   1 vegetable bouillon cube
>   1 cup all-purpose or raw cream
>   ¼ tsp. nutmeg
>   2 Tbs. fresh butter (optional)

Sauté the mushrooms in a heavy skillet and set them aside.

Prepare the cream sauce. In a heavy saucepan, melt the 2 Tbs. butter and stir in the flour. Add the water and the vegetable bouillon and bring to a boil, stirring constantly to dissolve the bouillon and thicken the sauce. Slowly stir in the cream and heat to thicken, stirring constantly. Do not boil. Add the nutmeg; stir well. Combine the Basic Sautéed Mushrooms with the cream sauce and set the mixture aside to cool while you prepare the crepes.

Heat a small frying pan and brush it lightly with butter. Pour approximately ¼ cup of batter into the center of the pan, immediately turning the pan so that the batter coats the entire bottom. Let the crepe set for just a few moments and turn it out onto a plate. When all the crepes have been prepared, place a few spoonfuls of the filling (not too much cream sauce) in the center of each, roll them tightly, and arrange them in a lightly buttered casserole dish. Pour the remaining sauce over the top. Dot with butter and place the crepes under the broiler for 5 minutes. Crepes combine well with a large green salad with Real French Dressing.

COLD RUSSIAN BEET SOUP

   2 bunches large beets
      Fresh-squeezed juice of 1 small lemon
   1 Tbs. honey
  12 small new or White Rose potatoes
   2 cucumbers
   2 pints sour cream

This beet soup should be prepared well in advance in order for it to chill thoroughly.

Trim off the greens and scrub the beets with a brush. Place them in a large soup pot and add water to cover. Bring to a boil and simmer until the beets are tender when pierced with a sharp knife, approximately ½ hour. Allow the beets to cool in the water. Remove them from the pot, reserving the liquid. Peel the beets and grate them on a coarse grater into the reserved liquid. Add the lemon juice. In a separate small pot, heat ¼ cup of the beet liquid, add the honey, and stir until it is dissolved. Return this sweetened mixture to the soup, stir thoroughly, and chill well for several hours or overnight.

One half hour before serving, steam the potatoes until tender in the top of a vegetable steamer. Peel and dice the cucumbers and set them aside. Add 1 cup of sour cream to the cold soup and mix thoroughly.

To serve, place two or three piping hot potatoes, cut into quarters, in each of four large soup bowls. Ladle the ice cold soup over the hot potatoes. Add the diced cucumber, allowing about half a cucumber per person. Place a large dollop of sour cream over all and pass additional sour cream to taste.

Beet soup, with its contrasting ingredients, is hearty and filling. Serve it as a main dish with Crusty Garlic Toast or fresh rye toast and a spinach and mushroom salad. Your guests will rave! Serves 4.

CRUSTY GARLIC TOAST

　3　cloves garlic
½　cup softened butter
12　slices whole grain bread

Preheat the broiler. Use a garlic press to crush the garlic into a bowl. Add the softened butter and beat together well with a fork. Smear the garlic butter on each slice of bread and arrange the slices on a broiler pan. Place under the heat for 5 minutes until the bread is toasted golden but not overly brown. Cool slightly and cut each slice in half diagonally. Serves 6 to 8.

STUFFED SQUASH

One Thanksgiving we craved stuffing but were not particularly interested in being involved in the turkey slaughter that takes place at that time of year. One day while we were shopping, we found an extremely large Turkish squash, which looks like a butternut but is much, much larger. When we cut the squash open, we found an immense cavity, full of seeds. Once the seeds were removed this was the obvious place for our stuffing. This dish can be part of a holiday buffet with Succotash Turnovers or French Vegetable Crescent, hot Honey Corn Bread, and a lovely big salad. This kind of holiday meal is such a vast departure from the traditional ones that it is a great treat. It is elegant and festive, but still properly combined and easily digested.

  1 large Turkish squash, or any extremely large squash that is
    not too watery
 12 slices whole grain bread
 ½ cup fresh butter
  1 stalk celery
  1 onion
  1 clove garlic (optional)
 ½ tsp. dried sage
 ¼ tsp. thyme
 ¼ tsp. bouquet garni
    Seasoned salt or salt-free seasoning to taste
  1 vegetable bouillon cube
 ½ cup boiling water

Open a large Turkish squash, lengthwise, and scrape the seeds out of the cavity. Set the squash aside while you prepare the stuffing.

Place the bread slices on a large cookie sheet and set it in the oven at 400 degrees for 15 to 20 minutes. This will dry the bread out, and the stuffing will hold together better.

Meanwhile, melt the butter in a large, heavy saucepan. Chop the celery and the onion and mince the garlic and add them to the melted butter. Sauté over medium-low heat until the celery is soft and the onion is transparent. Cut the bread into small cubes and add it to the vegetables. Sauté, stirring frequently for a few minutes, coating the bread with the melted butter. Add the sage, thyme, bouquet garni, and seasoned salt. Dissolve the vegetable bouillon in the boiling water and add it to the stuffing, taking care to moisten all the ingredients. Mix well.

Now you are ready to stuff the squash. Preheat the oven to 350 degrees. Fill both cavities as full as possible. Gently place the two halves back together and tie the squash tightly closed with kitchen cord. Place the squash in a large roasting pan or a shallow ovenproof casserole, if you have one large enough. Bake it for 1½ hours or until the squash is very soft.

To serve, remove the string and open the squash, fluffing up the stuffing with a fork. The squash can be transferred to a large platter or left in the casserole and served this way, or you can scoop it and the stuffing out of the shell and mix them together in a large serving bowl. The combination of flavors mixed together is exceptional. This stuffed squash serves 4 to 6 people as a main course, 8 to 10 people as a side dish.

THE BEANLESS BURRITO

Although we call this rice- and vegetable-stuffed tortilla a burrito, it actually resembles a burrito only in the way it is wrapped. Whenever I prepare this dish, I make a very large quantity. These are light, and people can eat a lot of them. They are also terrific cold the day after.

    2 cups steamed brown rice
    2 Tbs. safflower oil
    1 small onion, finely chopped
    2 cups finely chopped carrots
    2 cups chopped cauliflower
    1 cup fresh or frozen peas
    2 cups chopped bok choy leaves or cabbage
    2 cups chopped mushrooms (optional)
  ¼ tsp. oregano
    3 Tbs. soy sauce
    1 cup water
    3 Tbs. tahini
  12 whole wheat tortillas or chapatis

Prepare the brown rice, following the recipe for Perfect Brown Rice. Heat the safflower oil in a large saucepan. Add the onion and sauté to soften. Add the carrots and sauté. Add the cauliflower, peas, bok choy or cabbage, and mushrooms *one at a time,* sautéing briefly after each addition. Sauté the mixture together for 5 to 10 minutes or until all the vegetables begin to soften. Add the oregano, soy sauce, and water, bring to a boil, cover, and steam over low heat until the vegetables are tender, approximately 10 minutes. When the vegetables are ready and the brown rice has finished steaming, combine the two and stir in the tahini. The tahini helps to hold the whole mixture together.

Now you are ready to assemble the burritos. In a hot, dry frying pan, heat the tortillas one at a time for a few seconds on either side. Do not allow them to crisp. Place the hot tortilla on a piece of plastic wrap approximately 12 inches long. At this point you can smear a little softened fresh butter on the tortilla, if you wish. Place 5 or 6 heaping Tbs. of the rice-vegetable filling in the center of the tortillas. Fold the sides in and then roll the tortilla around the filling. Wrap the burrito tightly in the plastic wrap, and then repeat the process with the rest of the tortillas.

The burritos are easiest to keep and to serve if you leave them in the plastic wrap. This is a terrific party meal and can be prepared well in advance or even the day before. All that is needed with it is a large salad, or if it is part of a buffet, you can include Pea and Carrot Salad and Cream of Broccoli Soup or Dairyless Corn Chowder.

VEGETABLE TEMPURA

There are many different vegetables that can be used in tempura. Carrots, broccoli, string beans, sweet potatoes, zucchini are but a few of the possibilities. If you are using a flowery vegetable like broccoli, keep your tempura batter on the thin side. For carrots and string beans and other smooth vegetables, it can be thicker and creamier. Vegetable Tempura is a delicious accompaniment to a soup and salad meal. An unusual and surprisingly delicious tempura is carrot.

    1 egg, beaten
    2 cups whole wheat pastry flour
    ½ tsp. sea salt
  2½ cups ice water
       Several carrots or lbs. of carrots, depending on the
       number of people
    1 qt. unrefined safflower oil

Mix the first four ingredients together to make the batter, and keep it cold while you slice the carrots. For this tempura, the carrots must be sliced long and very thin. Cut each carrot into 3-inch sections. Cut each section in thin lengthwise slices. Then cut each slice into long, thin pieces, slightly thicker than matchsticks.

When all the carrots are sliced (there should be a large quantity, because this disappears fast when you put it on the table), heat the oil in a large wok. The oil is hot enough when a drop of the batter sizzles instantly. Place some of the carrots in the batter and then transfer them with a slotted spoon to the hot oil. They will sink and slowly rise to the top as they fry. When they are on the top and golden brown, remove them to drain on paper towels. Serve the tempura hot with bowls of tamari, soy sauce, or Chinese Salad Dressing.

Follow the same process with any other vegetable you wish to try. Tempura broccoli flowerettes. Cut zucchini in finger-length slices and use rounds of sweet potatoes or yams. Try onion rings, mushroom caps, or string beans. Usually not more than three vegetables are in tempura at any one meal.

VEGETABLE EGG ROLLS

Prepare your egg roll filling well in advance so it is cool and easy to handle when you are ready to wrap.

  2   bunches scallions
  3   carrots
 20   Japanese snow peas
  4   stalks bok choy
  2   Tbs. unrefined safflower oil
  6   cups fresh bean sprouts
 ½   cup boiling water
  1   vegetable bouillon cube
  4   Tbs. soy sauce
  1   tsp. cornstarch or arrowroot
  2   Tbs. cold water
 ¼   tsp. garlic powder
  1   Tbs. brown rice vinegar (optional)
  1   package egg roll skins
  1   tsp. raw honey (optional)
  1   qt. unrefined safflower oil

Prepare the vegetables. Cut the scallions in lengthwise thin slices. Cut the carrots into small (pea-sized) cubes. Julienne the snow peas and finely chop the bok choy, using the green leaf. Heat the 2 Tbs. of oil in a large, heavy saucepan or in a wok. Add the scallions and stir fry. Add the carrots and the snow peas. Stir fry for several minutes after each addition. Add the bok choy, stir fry a bit longer, and finally add the bean sprouts. Mix the vegetables well to combine them. Add the ½ cup of boiling water in which you have dissolved the vegetable bouillon. Add 2 Tbs. of the soy sauce, mix well, cover, and steam for approximately 5 minutes or until the vegetables are fairly soft. The vegetables do not have to be completely cooked because they will continue to cook inside the egg roll. Mix together the cornstarch, cold water, garlic powder, rice vinegar, honey, and remaining 2 Tbs. of the soy sauce, and add it to the vegetables. Bring to a boil and stir until the sauce is quite thick. This filling must not be runny. Cool.

Now you are ready to make the egg rolls. Have on hand a small bowl of cold water for sealing the edges. Place an ample amount of filling in an egg roll skin. The amount you use will depend on whether you want your egg rolls to be thin or fat. Roll the egg rolls from edge to edge, folding in the sides first, or from corner to corner. Seal the outer edge by moistening it with a little water. Set each egg roll aside as you roll it, and when they are all rolled heat the oil in a large wok. The oil is ready when a drop of water in it sizzles. Gently place four or five egg rolls in the hot oil. They will sink to the bottom and then begin to rise as they fry. When each egg roll is a golden brown, remove it to drain on paper towel. Be sure to drain them well so that they will not be oily. This amount yields approximately 18 delicious egg rolls.

EASY CHOW MEIN

½ lb. any whole wheat spaghetti (Japanese noodles such as brown rice udon, buckwheat soba, or jinenjo noodles are all delicious for this dish)
½ lb. (3 cups) long mung bean sprouts
2 Tbs. light soy sauce
2 Tbs. tamari
1 Tbs. white or yellow miso
½ tsp. roasted sesame oil (optional)
2 Tbs. unrefined safflower oil
1 medium onion, sliced
4 cups bok choy greens, coarsely shredded
½ tsp. sea salt, seasoned salt, or salt-free seasoning to taste
  Freshly ground pepper to taste

Cook the noodles according to package directions. Rinse under cold water and set aside. Blanch the sprouts in boiling water for 1 minute. Drain well and set aside. Heat a wok over medium-high heat. Combine the soy sauce, tamari, miso, and sesame oil and set aside. Add the safflower oil to the wok and swirl to coat the sides. Add the onion and stir fry until it begins to turn transparent. Add the bok choy greens and stir fry until they begin to turn bright green. Add the noodles and toss well. Add the bean sprouts and continue tossing to combine. Pour the sauce over the mixture and toss well. Season with salt and freshly ground pepper, if desired. Serves 4 to 6.

7

IMPORTANT REMINDERS

The Simple Fundamental Principles

Drink fresh fruit and vegetable juices on an empty stomach. Eat fruit alone, on an empty stomach. Have a salad meal every day. Combine foods properly. Eat high-water-content foods. Use only pure, fresh, unrefined ingredients. Make each meal a healthy, happy, joyous experience.

IMPORTANT REMINDERS

Now that you have come through the entire guide book for your journey to HEALTH, you have at your disposal a large amount of new information. Remember the importance of drinking juices. Learn to substitute these for any other beverages you may now be drinking. By consciously partaking of energizing fruit juices and nourishing vegetable juices, you can teach your body to crave these beverages, rather than coffee, tea, alcohol, or other addictive drinks.

Remember to eat fruit alone, *on an empty stomach.* Fruit and its juices will cleanse your body of the excess weight you wish to lose. It will cleanse your skin of unsightly blemishes. You will lose that tired look and begin to shine.

Learn to depend on salad—its high water content is second only to that of fruit. Become a salad addict. Have a salad every day, and learn to use salads to overcome cravings for heavier foods that you may be having.

Remember to combine foods properly. Eat fruit alone. If you are having a heavy protein, combine it with salad or steamed vegetables. If you are having a heavy carbohydrate, combine *it* with vegetables or salad. *Avoid combining proteins and carbohydrates.* Such combinations result in an acute slowing of the digestive processes and make it difficult to lose weight or improve your health.

Use the purest ingredients available in preparing your

meals. Avoid all refined and chemically treated foods. Use fresh fruits and fresh vegetables, rather than canned or frozen ones. Avoid white sugar, white flour, and white rice.

Experiment with the recipes herein. Feel free to substitute vegetables and grains of your choice for the ones that are suggested. One of the advantages of a healthful diet is its flexibility. You are not trapped in any prescribed regimen. You can make use of seasonal changes and your own cravings in determining what you will eat. Take advantage of the vast varieties of salads and develop others of your own. Use the transition diet meals when it is necessary for you to eat foods that are heavier than salad. And by all means, enjoy the feasting chapter. The menus and ideas it contains are there for the express purpose of satisfying your heavier cravings.

I hope I have helped to make eating a healthier and more pleasurable experience for you.

For further information about FIT FOR LIFE projects, please send your name and address to Harvey and Marilyn Diamond, 2210 Wilshire Blvd., Suite 118, Santa Monica, CA 90403 and we will put you on our mailing list.

"MAY EVERY DAY OF YOUR LIFE BE HEALTHIER
THAN THE DAY BEFORE."

INDEX